T0319026

Cambridge Elements ≣

Elements in Perception
edited by
James T. Enns
The University of British Columbia

ELEMENTS OF SCENE PERCEPTION

Monica S. Castelhano
Queen's University

Carrick C. Williams
California State University San Marcos

CAMBRIDGE
UNIVERSITY PRESS

CAMBRIDGE
UNIVERSITY PRESS

University Printing House, Cambridge CB2 8BS, United Kingdom

One Liberty Plaza, 20th Floor, New York, NY 10006, USA

477 Williamstown Road, Port Melbourne, VIC 3207, Australia

314–321, 3rd Floor, Plot 3, Splendor Forum, Jasola District Centre,
New Delhi – 110025, India

103 Penang Road, #05–06/07, Visioncrest Commercial, Singapore 238467

Cambridge University Press is part of the University of Cambridge.

It furthers the University's mission by disseminating knowledge in the pursuit of
education, learning, and research at the highest international levels of excellence.

www.cambridge.org
Information on this title: www.cambridge.org/9781108932714
DOI: 10.1017/9781108924092

First published 2021

A catalogue record for this publication is available from the British Library.

ISBN 978-1-108-93271-4 Paperback
ISSN 2515-0502 (online)
ISSN 2515-0499 (print)

Elements of Scene Perception

Elements in Perception

DOI: 10.1017/9781108924092
First published online: October 2021

Monica S. Castelhano
Queen's University

Carrick C. Williams
California State University San Marcos

Author for correspondence: Monica S. Castelhano, monica.castelhano@queensu.ca

Abstract: Visual cognitive processes have traditionally been examined with simplified stimuli, but generalization of these processes to the real world is not always straightforward. Using images, computer-generated images, and virtual environments, researchers have examined processing of visual information in the real world. Although referred to as scene perception, this research field encompasses many aspects of scene processing. Beyond the perception of visual features, scene processing is fundamentally influenced and constrained by semantic information as well as spatial layout and spatial associations with objects. In this Element, we will present recent advances in how scene processing occurs within a few seconds of exposure, how scene information is retained in the long term, and how different tasks affect attention in scene processing. By considering the characteristics of real-world scenes, as well as different time windows of processing, we can develop a fuller appreciation of the research that falls under the wider umbrella of scene processing.

Keywords: scene perception, visual attention, eye movements, visual memory, spatial processing

ISBNs: 9781108932714 (PB), 9781108924092 (OC)
ISSNs: 2515-0502 (online), 2515-0499 (print)

Contents

1 Introduction

When you are walking from your bedroom to your kitchen, processing of your environment includes the layout of the furniture, recognizing items in each of those rooms, and even the types of tasks we do in each of those places (Castelhano & Heaven, 2011; Castelhano & Henderson, 2007, 2008b; Castelhano & Witherspoon, 2016; Henderson, 2003; Torralba et al., 2006; Williams & Castelhano, 2019). Scene perception seems seamless and effortless, belying many of the underlying processes that occur so that we can understand, interact with, and navigate everyday environments that vary in their content and scope (see Figure 1). We can also see how all these processes interact when we go grocery shopping and have a list of items to collect around that space. Not only do you need to navigate to the correct area of the supermarket, but you also need to distinguish among different types of items when you get there and choose an item based on any number of discriminating factors (Castelhano & Heaven, 2010; Castelhano & Henderson, 2003; Castelhano & Krzyś, 2020; Fernandes & Castelhano, 2021; Man et al., 2019). Another way to think about how we interact with scenes is not just within a single indoor space, but spaces as we explore different places. For instance, navigating in a new city is markedly different from navigating to a location that is highly familiar, such as a daily commute to work or class (Barhorst-Cates et al., 2016; Castelhano, Pollatsek, et al., 2009; Castelhano & Krzyś, 2020; Castelhano & Pollatsek, 2010; Epstein & Baker, 2019; Maguire et al., 2016). The arrays of different types of information available from the visual environment and how these are used across tasks demonstrate the complexity of scene perception and are as varied as the properties of scenes themselves (see Figure 1).

Even from a few examples, such as thinking about navigating a supermarket, we can easily see many ways in which scene perception as an area of research is a misnomer. Beyond the initial perceptual processing, scene perception research encompasses different types of processing of real-world environments, including attention, eye-movement guidance, memory, effects on other types of processing (i.e., context effects on object recognition), and spatial processing. Because of the complexity and enormity of the scene-processing literature, it is helpful to divide up the work into various sections. Here, we use the information-processing timeline and start with early perceptual processes before moving on to more complex and elaborate processing of scenes and space. We describe each of these, along with a summary of the six main sections of the Element (Initial Scene Understanding; Online Scene Representations; Long-Term Memory for Scenes; Eye Movements and Scenes; Searching through Scenes; and Spatial Representations and Navigation).

Figure 1 Different types of scenes are illustrated across example images. On the left-hand side are indoor scenes and on the right are outdoor scenes, which can be natural landscapes, cityscapes, or a combination of human-made and natural.

Think back to when you have been quickly scrolling through a streaming video service, where you only have a snapshot of each show in the form of an image. To choose, you have to quickly identify the image to determine if something looks interesting. In Section 2 we will examine how scenes are initially perceived and identified. If we use the processing timeline as a guide, scene perception begins with questions about how scenes are initially processed. In fact, when we think of scene perception, the first thing that comes to mind is how we are able to initially assess and understand the world around us. This is perhaps why the term is such a misnomer as these questions were first asked in the literature and the name persisted. This section will review what seemed at first like instantaneous processing, but is now understood as very fast processing that is thought to occur in a fraction of a second (Biederman, 1972;

Castelhano & Henderson, 2008a; Castelhano & Pollatsek, 2010; Goffaux et al., 2005; Greene & Oliva, 2009a, 2009b; Oliva & Schyns, 1997; Potter, 1976; Schyns & Oliva, 1994).

Going about the day, as we move around and do different tasks, the environment, and thus our representation of the environment, changes – in discreet as well as significant ways. In Section 3, we will examine the ways in which online representation was originally conceptualized and how this theoretical framework and tool is viewed today in light of more recent findings. While the notion that different types of information are prioritized across space and time when examining a scene is not new, it has implications for the ongoing representation of visual information as we view a scene.

Based on how information is prioritized for further scrutiny, researchers have also examined how information is represented from moment to moment (i.e., online representation). Online representation arises from a basic information-processing model of cognition, where information from the real world is acquired and reconstructed in the mind. Initially, the reconstruction of the world was thought to be quite veridical, such that we had an accurate and complete portrayal and understanding of the visual world around us. It is interesting that the importance of the internal representation is highlighted also in reference to eye movements. Because of the structure and mechanics of the eye, we see with high acuity only at the location to which the eyes are directly pointed; and yet, our perception of the world is that it is stable, ever present, and highly detailed across the whole of the visual field. This juxtaposition is solved with the notion of a veridical or, at the very least, highly accurate internal presentation of the world. While we are focused on one region, the representation supports the perception that the whole of the visual world is present in high detail. While intuitively appealing, this view was deemed to be impossibly difficult to compute (Gilman, 1994; Warren, 2012). We consider these and other approaches to how to think about scene representations that support perception and tasks in the moment in this third section.

After being in a space for some time and then leaving it, there is a question of how much of the information of the space and objects remains. Section 4 will examine the various points of view on how information is stored in memory. Building on the information prioritized in the moment and then held onto as a person explores a scene, researchers have also examined how information from scenes is stored in long-term memory. Much like online representations, researchers initially assumed that long-term representations (information kept in memory once a person has left a room or stopped viewing a room) were quite rich. This was supported by a number of studies showing how briefly viewed scenes could be recognized with high accuracy for some time (Potter, 1976;

Potter & Levy, 1969), even when the number of scenes held in memory was in the thousands (Mandler & Johnson, 1976; Shepard, 1967; Standing, 1973). This amazing feat of memory was thought to be possible only with highly detailed memory. Interestingly, while the notion did come under fire for some time, new research has once again swung the pendulum back – and shown that the information retained in long-term memory is more detailed (Konkle et al., 2010; Konkle & Brady, 2010). The nuance is now in how different details of the scene are more memorable, and how these different details lead to differences in retention of information over time. This fourth section will address how recent studies have shed further light on the nuances of different types of information represented in memory.

When walking down a city street, ads are looking to attract your attention from billboards, bus shelters, and posters stuck on walls and poles. Distractedly, you can feel yourself drawn to the images and words, or when you are focused on a task at hand (e.g., checking a text or driving), they can be utterly ignored. Section 5 will examine the influence of various sources of information on the allocation of attention and eye movements. Research into how attention is allocated is governed by the notion that attention was either pulled to attractive/distinctive regions (bottom-up influences) or pushed to useful or task-relevant regions (top-down influences). When examining the role of these different influences, eye movements indicate where and when a person is paying attention to different aspects of the scene and are an important tool in this research. This fifth section will review attentional processes and how eye movements can tell us something about them.

A simple task like making a cheese and cucumber sandwich requires us to locate and assemble the different components. This searching, whether for ingredients or tools, lies at the heart of so many tasks, and yet there are still a lot of questions about how we go about doing this successfully. Section 6 will examine how the various aspects of a scene affect performance, and how traditional notions of context can be broken down into different types of influences from the larger context. The interaction of information prioritized for further scrutiny and the information contained within the online representation is best encapsulated by the visual search task. In a visual search task, participants are given a target and then asked to locate it within the scene as quickly as possible. Traditionally, visual search tasks were investigated using arrays of shapes, but when searching in scenes, visual search performance is also affected by other factors (Castelhano & Heaven, 2011; Castelhano & Pereira, 2018; Loftus & Mackworth, 1978; Malcolm & Henderson, 2010; Võ & Henderson, 2011). This sixth section will examine these different factors influencing visual search and how it has evolved over the last decade.

Although most research to date has examined scene perception while participants are viewing scenes, we know that in our daily lives we process scene information while standing in them (Castelhano & Krzyś, 2020; Castelhano & Witherspoon, 2016; Gibson, 1979). Section 7 will examine how scene processing is influenced by spatial aspects of information. Research examining these aspects of scenes faces new and interesting problems and constraints. For instance, the spatial arrangement of structures and objects has to be kept in mind even when not in full view, as some of the information is behind the viewer. For this reason, many researchers have examined scene processing across viewpoints (Castelhano et al., 2008; Castelhano & Pollatsek, 2010; Epstein et al., 2003, 2005; Garsoffky et al., 2002; Li et al., 2016) and across different views of panoramic images (Garsoffky et al., 2002; Park et al., 2010). This seventh section will cover different aspects of spatial scene processing, from across different views and when incorporating information into a larger representation that extends beyond the current view.

Overall, in addition to examining a number of theoretical research domains in which the study of scene processing has been led, the current review will also look at how this research is applied to real-world examples. The "Application in the Real World" presented at the end of each section will highlight one example of how these fundamental questions about processing influence our understanding of other tasks and events. For instance, we will explore real-world problems such as how an advertisement is looked at, the veracity of eyewitness memory of a scene, the performance of radiologists in detecting problems in an x-ray, and the impact of pictures on the acceptance of fake news. The extensive research in scene processing can give insights into how these tasks operate, as well as the limitations of human performance under those task demands.

2 Initial Scene Understanding

Early studies showed how quickly information from real-world scenes could be understood. In a now seminal study, Potter (1976) showed participants a rapid sequence of briefly presented, unrelated images (referred to as Rapid Serial Visual Presentation or RSVP) and asked them before or after the sequence whether an image was present in the stream. Images were shown for as little as 113 ms each, mimicking a brief fixation on the image. The results revealed that when given a label for an image prior to viewing the stream of images, participants could easily identify the target image; however, when given the label afterwards, they could not. Together, the findings led to the conclusion that although images could quickly be processed to the point of interpretation and understanding, the memory of that information is fleeting without additional time to consolidate it.

Potter's (1976) study was in line with other studies from that time that explored not only how quickly images were understood but also to what extent different types of information drove this rapid understanding (Biederman, 1972; Friedman, 1979; Loftus & Mackworth, 1978; Shepard, 1967). Based on research from the memory literature, Friedman (1979) proposed that scene representations are initially formed by an inference made based on the perceived objects, which were largely held to be the basic semantic unit of the scene across a number of studies (Biederman, 1972; Friedman, 1979; Loftus & Mackworth, 1978; Shepard, 1967). The rapid understanding of scenes found in Potter (1976), however, spurred researchers to move away from the notion of the object as the basic unit of understanding and to examine how different visual features contribute.

To examine how different aspects of the scene were perceived over time, Fei Fei Li and colleagues (Li et al., 2007) had participants view images for various durations (from an extremely brief 27 ms to a longer exposure of 500 ms). Based on this view, participants would then write a description of what they saw in the image. These open-ended responses allowed the researchers to extract and organize different descriptors into a hierarchical tree of attributes. Analysis of the responses showed that with longer durations, specific objects were included in the description as well as whole narrations as to what event the image may have captured. In contrast, with very brief exposures to the image, many of the descriptors centered on perceptual features, colors, and shapes. This focus on visual features is how many researchers have approached the initial processing of scenes and how they lead to the identification of the image. We turn to these studies next.

While examining basic visual features and their contribution to scene understanding, one notion that has been debated is which feature provides crucial information for identification: color vs. spatial frequencies. Both color and spatial frequency information are processed in the early visual cortex and are thought to be the basic components used to derive a visual representation of the environment (Castelhano & Henderson, 2008b; Greene & Oliva, 2009b; Larson & Loschky, 2009; Nijboer et al., 2008; Oliva & Schyns, 2000; Oliva & Torralba, 2001). Spatial frequency information is thought to convey scene structure information, with larger shapes conveyed by lower frequency and details and edges conveyed in high-frequency information (see Figure 2). Thus, either component (or both) could be used to derive identifying information when a scene image is first viewed.

Researchers have debated for some time whether the rapid understanding of scene images is driven by the color in scene images or edge-based contours

Low Spatial Frequency

High Spatial Frequency

Course-to-Fine

Figure 2 The same image shown with low spatial frequencies only (left side) and high spatial frequencies only (right side). Different spatial frequency bands are thought to convey different aspects of the scene, but all convey some information about the scene structure. See text for more details.

(Bacon-Mace et al., 2005; Biederman, 1988; Biederman & Ju, 1988; Castelhano & Henderson, 2008b; Delorme et al., 2000; Goffaux et al., 2005; Macé et al., 2010; Oliva & Schyns, 1997, 2000; Schyns & Oliva, 1994). Biederman (Biederman, 1988; Biederman & Ju, 1988) argued that because the information processing occurred so quickly, only contours and edges had an influence on initial scene processing, while color contributed minimally.

Further research into the contribution of edges and contours has shown that they are sufficient to support scene understanding. For instance, Schyns and Oliva (Oliva & Schyns, 1997; Schyns & Oliva, 1994) had participants identify hybrid images. Hybrid images were composites of two photographic images – one that occupied a low spatial frequency range (seen only as blurry contours) and another that occupied a high spatial frequency range (seen only as sharp edges and detailed textures). In an initial study, Schyns and Oliva (1994) found that when the hybrid images were briefly presented (~50 ms), participants tended to categorize the image in the low-frequency more readily than the high-frequency range. With longer exposures (~100 ms), this pattern flipped such that the high-frequency image was categorized more readily than the low-frequency image. Based on this pattern of results, the researchers concluded that image processing proceeds from blurred to more detailed image properties. However, in a follow-up study they used an implicit training method, such that images were presented rapidly either at high or low frequency (with the complementary frequencies presenting as white noise). This training encouraged participants to attend to either the high- or low-frequency image information exclusively, as the white noise did not offer any useful information. After training, participants were then shown the true hybrid images (with an image presented at each of the high- and low-frequency ranges) for both short and longer exposure durations. They found that participants tended to report the category of the image at the frequency range in which they were trained – in other words, both high and low image information were available at short exposure durations. This finding threw new light on previous results, as it was not the case that high-frequency information was not available at shorter exposure durations or took longer to process; instead, the progress of processing information from blurred to more detailed image properties was a mere preference or default of the system. Thus, the progression in how visual features from real-world images are processed and have an influence is not fixed, but rather subject to influences and changes due to tasks and circumstances.

Although many researchers have concentrated on how spatial frequencies and edge information contribute to the initial understanding of scene images, others have been interested in the possible contributions of color. As mentioned earlier, many early studies showed no evidence that color contributed to the understanding of scenes – or rather that there was no discernible cost to presenting images without color (Codispoti et al., 2012; Delorme et al., 2000; Yao & Einhauser, 2008). For instance, Delorme et al. (2000) had participants classify images as to whether they contained fruit or an animal presented briefly (~32 ms). They showed images in both full color and grayscale (black-and-white images). They found that classification of images was only mildly impaired when color information was removed and concluded that color was not used to make these classification decisions.

The findings with scene images seemed in complete contradiction to many studies that examined the recognition of individual objects, which did find a benefit from color (Joseph & Proffitt, 1996; Mapelli & Behrmann, 1997; Price & Humphreys, 1989; Tanaka & Presnell, 1999). For instance, in one study, Tanaka and Presnell (1999) had participants categorize pictures of objects that were either in expected or unexpected colors. Importantly, they made a distinction between high-diagnostic objects, which are those that are highly associated with a specific color (e.g., a banana), and low-diagnostic objects, which are not associated with a specific color (e.g., a lamp). They found that when high-diagnostic objects were shown in colors other than the expected ones (monochrome or incongruent colors), performance was negatively affected. However, there were no effects on performance when low-diagnostic objects were shown in the different color conditions. They concluded that color does have an effect on the initial processing of objects, but only in certain cases – where there is an association between the object and its semantic category.

The results from the object recognition literature seem to contradict what was found in the scene literature, especially because scenes were largely conceptualized as collections of spatially arranged objects. One important difference between the studies examining contributions of color in scene images and in objects was in how and whether the color was linked to the semantic representation of the visual information being depicted. One approach to examining the contribution of color was to examine how it affected scene categories that were associated with specific colors (Castelhano & Henderson, 2008b; Castelhano & Rayner, 2008; Gegenfurtner & Rieger, 2000; Oliva & Schyns, 2000; Spence et al., 2006; Wichmann et al., 2002). In one study, Oliva and Schyns (2000) examined whether color had an important influence on scene perception when the scene colors were diagnostic of the scene category (see Figure 3). They had participants categorize scene images that were presented either in full color, no color, or abnormal colors. The abnormal colors were defined as those on the opposite side of the color space, such that each hue was swapped with its opposite (e.g., blues for yellows, etc.). Importantly, scene categories were distinct in the color space they occupied, such that

Figure 3 The images based on the different color conditions used in Oliva and Schyns (2000). They include (A) normal color, (B) abnormal color, and (C) monochrome images.

none of the color-diagnostic categories overlapped (e.g., coast, canyon, desert, forest). They found that not only were the colored images categorized more quickly than the no color images, but there was also a cost for images presented with abnormal colors. Oliva and Schyns conclude that for certain scene categories that are associated with a specific color space, color does contribute to the initial understanding of those images.

In another study, Castelhano and Henderson (2008) also investigated contributions of color to initial scene perceptions by examining whether the structure of the scene modulated the effectiveness of color contributions. They compared colored and grayscale images that were presented either with a full range of spatial frequencies (normal images) or with high spatial frequency removed (blurred images; see Figure 4). They found that when presented normally, there was no additional improvement in performance when images were presented in color over grayscale. However, when images were blurred, there was a significant improvement in performance for colored images over grayscale ones. Further experiments examined whether the color in blurred images was merely helping to define structure in the blurred images. When blurred images were also shown in abnormal colors there was no corresponding benefit in

Figure 4 The presentation of images in normal (A, B) and low frequency (C, D), in color (A, C) and monochrome (B, D). Taken with permission from Castelhano and Henderson (2008).

performance. In contrast, the color helped to activate the correct scene category when the structural information was not as accessible.

When comparing detailed visual properties and global scene properties, Greene and Oliva (2009a) found that when viewed very briefly (30 ms), scenes tend to be classified by global information rather than local information even when the classification is performed on semantic scene categories. Responses to scenes possessing global properties of scenes (e.g., openness, temperature) that were indicative of the semantic scene category (e.g., forest), but were not part of that category themselves, were more likely to be false alarms than those that did not share those global properties. In addition, people can adapt to a particular global property by experiencing many instances of that property, leading to aftereffects on other stimuli (Greene & Oliva, 2010). Thus, extraction of scene information occurs rapidly and from a number of local and global features, which are flexibly examined depending on the availability of those properties in the stimulus.

3 Online Scene Representations

When looking at a scene, there is an impression that the entire scene is equally visible at all times and there is substantial visual data available across the whole visual field. However, the reality of the visual world does not match that impression. The structure of the retina means that only the central 2° of visual angle (corresponding to the fovea) is processed to the highest acuity (Rayner, 2009). The remainder of the visual world loses acuity rapidly as one moves away from the fovea and into the periphery of the retina. The fact that the impression of the visual world is one that is completely accessible is what is called the "grand illusion" in vision research; information about a scene is not universally available, but it seems to be. Why would such an impression exist?

The grand illusion points to limits of online scene representations, but we can and do represent scenes as we view them. Potter (1976) demonstrated that scene information can be extracted rapidly and compared to a label. As mentioned earlier, Potter presented a description of a scene (either a picture or a verbal description) and then presented a series of images in rapid succession (as many as eight images per second). Participants indicated if a scene matching the description was in the sequence (a separate group tried to memorize the sequence). She found that detection rates were greater than 60 percent even in the fastest presentation sequence, indicating that participants were able to rapidly extract the critical information from a scene and compare it to a label. Although participants could identify the presence of a specified image in the stream even at the fastest rate, memorization took substantially longer per image. The difference between memorization and detection indicates that although scenes can be rapidly identified, the memory of the image is also susceptible to interference from subsequently presented images.

Given that scenes are available rapidly, what kind of information is extracted and used for representation? When examining the types of information that are available, the structure of the scene, the general meaning of the scene (as in Potter, 1976), and the objects within the scene are all viable candidates for elements that can build an online scene representation. Although each piece has been investigated separately, these components frequently interact. For example, the spatial layout and structure of the scene limits the locations where objects appear. Thus, although they are all separate pieces of information, it is important to remember that it is the interaction of these pieces of information that forms the representation.

As described earlier, scenes extend across height, width, and depth. Although most research performed on scenes has used two-dimensional images, it is understood that the image represents a three-dimensional reality. Intraub (2010) argued that scene representation was not purely visual. Instead, it is a multisource representation that takes into account other information than just the visual input. Intraub and colleagues (Intraub & Richardson, 1989; Intraub, 2010; Park et al., 2007) describe a phenomenon called boundary extension whereby a scene is remembered as containing more information than had actually been presented. The extension is thought to indicate that the scene representation includes not only what can be seen but also what is expected and/or predicted beyond the edges of the visual scene. Intraub describes how if one sees a set of garbage cans against a fence, one may also represent the areas to the sides or behind the viewer, making it difficult to remember exactly what was seen. Although it is a form of reality monitoring failure, this extension of the visible area into areas not actually seen would be a more holistic representation of the space (Intraub, 2010, 2012; Intraub et al., 1998). Although the scene representation can be thought of as extending beyond the visual scene, the vast majority of the research on scene representation emphasizes the visible area of the scene. Given that, we will focus on the visible scene and how the information in the visible area is represented. However, even with that limitation, there is a substantial amount of information that can be represented at any one time.

The spatial structure of a scene forms the foundation of a scene's representation. One of the critical factors of spatial information is the limitation that spatial information in a scene can have on the placement of objects. The layout and structure of the scene provide valuable information about the way that objects in the scene can exist. Although scenes are more than just an arrangement of objects, the objects themselves are critical to the representation of the scenes. Objects in a realistic scene have to conform to physical laws like gravity (described as syntax by Biederman, 1972). Objects do not float around unless one is in the microgravity climate of a space vessel.

The arrangement of objects in real-world scenes also provides for clustering of objects that have meaning. In many examinations of the visual search with real-world objects, for example, objects are placed randomly on a blank background with no concern for real-world physical laws or logical groupings (e.g., Hout & Goldinger, 2012; Williams, 2010; Williams et al., 2009; Wolfe, 2007). Rather than having objects that are evenly spread (e.g., Zelinsky et al., 1997), real-world scenes have groupings of objects that are meaningful and clustered. These clusters can help with understanding the content of the scene (Brooks et al., 2010; Castelhano et al., 2019; Pereira & Castelhano, 2012, 2014). For instance, Pereira and Castelhano (2014) found that object information could interact with scene context to guide the eyes to a search target. Using a moving window paradigm, they removed either the scene context or the object information from a scene (see Figure 5). They argued that scene context provides the scaffolding that helps guide attention to the general area, while the object information allows for more specific targeting of the object once within that area.

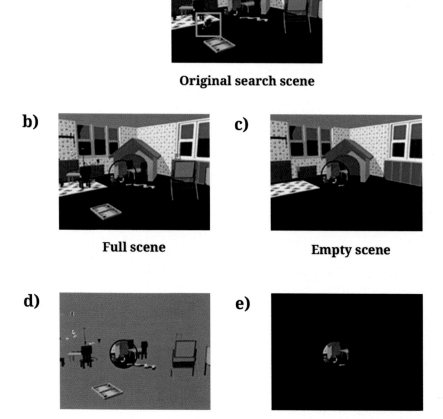

Figure 5 Although the full scene is shown here (with the target highlighted for illustrative purposes), this image (a) was presented at the gaze position, through a 2° radius gaze-contingent window that was centered on the fixation point. The scene context was manipulated outside this window in the periphery. The stimuli manipulation included scene context with some object (b), showing just the scene context (c), only objects (d), and no preview control (e). Taken with permission from Pereira and Castelhano (2014). See text for detail.

In an attempt to further integrate spatial and object information, Castelhano and colleagues (Castelhano & Krzyś, 2020; Pereira & Castelhano, 2019) proposed the Surface Guidance Framework, in order to understand the spatial structure of scenes. This framework indicates that the horizontal and vertical dimensions of a scene provide different types of information to the viewer (see

Figure 6). In the vertical dimension, there are bands that can relate to the ground level, midlevel, and upper portions of the scene. In these bands, there are surfaces (horizontal) where objects can exist. Objects have surfaces within a scene where they normally occur; objects that tend to appear on the ground rarely exist on the ceiling. By understanding the manner in which objects appear, scenes can be represented efficiently. For example, a desktop forms a horizontal surface in the midlevel vertical band. Objects that are expected to be on a desk (e.g., a computer monitor) would be unlikely to be on the floor or near the ceiling. Even without looking at the scene, one knows that the object is likely in the midlevel. In contrast, the exact position of the monitor on the horizontal surface is unknown. This is an example of the information about the scene's structure and the information about the objects in a scene interacting. This interaction will be further discussed in Section 6.

3.1 Change Blindness and the Grand Illusion

Beginning in the 1990s, a phenomenon was described that challenged the notion of what could be represented in a scene, going as far as to question whether any representation was needed at all. Grimes (1996) described a situation where large-scale changes could be made to a scene, if the change occurred during an eye movement, and the viewer would be unaware of them. In other words, people had *change blindness*. This idea harkens back to the work of McConkie and Zola (1979) who made changes to alternating case text (e.g., UpPeR aNd

Figure 6 Based on the Surface Guidance Framework, the different scene regions are associated with different types of targets. Top panel: examples of search scenes; bottom panel: highlighted surface regions (red = upper, yellow = middle, green = lower) as per the Surface Guidance Framework. Taken with permission from Pereira and Castelhano (2019). See text for more detail.

LoWeR would change to uPpEr AnD lOwEr) during eye movements and found that reading speed was unaffected. The finding by Grimes in picture stimuli challenges the notion that we can retain visual information form fixation to fixation. If large-scale changes in a scene can occur and be undetected, little information must be retained.

Following this demonstration, many investigations of change blindness occurred. Rensink, O'Regan, and Clark (1997) investigated the idea of change blindness with a new paradigm called the flicker paradigm. Instead of relying on the disruption of vision caused by a saccadic eye movement, the flicker paradigm involves inserting a visual disruption between the two versions of the changing image (the original and the changed version) that are alternated until the change is detected. In other words, a scene is presented, a disruption occurs, the changed scene is presented, another disruption occurs, and the sequence repeats (see Figure 7). The critical dependent variable is the time (or number of alternations) needed to detect the change. Rensink et al. (1997) found that changes to objects of central interest in an image were detected more quickly than those of marginal interest, indicating a powerful role of attention in detecting changes. Hollingworth and Henderson (2000) extended this notion, finding that changes to objects that were inconsistent with the overall scene context were easier to detect than changes that were consistent with the scene context. Thus, objects central to the image are more easily remembered, as are those that are inconsistent with the scene context.

To account for the demonstration of change blindness and the grand illusion overall, Rensink (2000) proposed that rather than trying to represent the entire scene, the viewer only held a solid representation of the currently attended object and everything else was murky. Called "coherence theory," Rensink argued that the difference in detecting changes across disruptions for central and marginal interest objects indicates that those objects were not represented in a complete form unless they were the focus of attention the moment the change occurred. If one were attending to an object when it changed, the change would be detected because there was a solid representation of the object to which to compare the changed image. Objects of central interest would be more likely to receive the attention (also sooner in viewing the scene) than objects of marginal interest and thus changes to them would be detected more quickly. Although the rest of the visual world is made up of unstable proto-objects that can be created and replaced rapidly, the current focus of attention is clear. When attention shifts to a new object, the new object coheres into a solid representation and the previously attended object reverts to a proto-object. Thus, wherever one is looking, the world appears complete and whole, but outside of that focus of attention, there is a sea of objects that can be replaced on a whim.

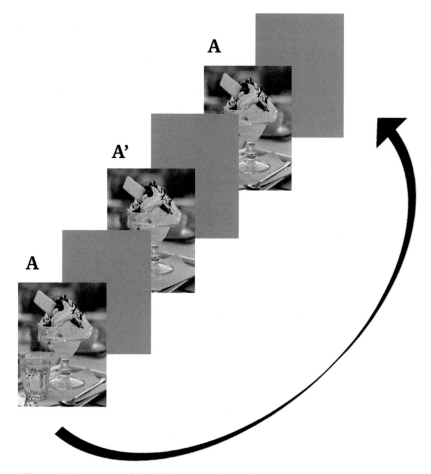

Figure 7 Sequence of the flicker paradigm. The trial progressed through two different images (A and A') that differed by one detail and a gray mask that obscured the change between the images. In this example the changing detail is the spoon.

In a follow-up discussion of these findings, O'Regan and Noë (2001) took this argument further by stating there is no need to represent the external visual world internally. They argue that it would be computationally costly to represent the visual world internally because of the number of things that have to be calculated and the fact that internal representation would constantly need to be updated with new information. It is unnecessary to represent the visual world internally; the visual world itself could serve as an outside visual memory. The visual system actively extracts information from the world all the time, and if one needs to "recall" what something looks like, all that is needed is to point the eyes to that location again. Therefore, there is no need to try to represent that information internally. The grand illusion is the result of the lack of a visual representation; there is nothing except what one is viewing with which to compare the representation. Because there is nothing represented, change blindness is a common if not constant state.

The grand illusion and coherence theory both point to a lack of visual information being stored outside the focus of attention. However, there have been several instances of visual information being retained even outside the focus of attention. Hollingworth and colleagues (Hollingworth, 2005; Hollingworth & Henderson, 2002; Hollingworth et al., 2001) present findings demonstrating the importance of a scene representation in memory beyond the most recently attended object. Hollingworth et al. (2001) had participants view scenes and indicate if a change occurred to any object. The change to an object (if one occurred) happened after the first time the eyes fixated the critical object. On the eye movement away from the critical object, the critical object was changed to another token of the same basic category. Because the change occurred after the object had been fixated, it was reasonably certain that the critical object had been the focus of attention, but it was no longer the focus. If no information is retained outside of attention, then changes to the critical object should be impossible to detect. Although change detection was poor, it exceeded the false alarm rate, indicating that participants were retaining the information even outside of the focus of attention. In addition, detection rates for the semantically inconsistent objects (e.g., a teddy bear in a science lab) were better than for semantically consistent objects (e.g., a microscope), indicating that the initial attention to those objects affected later detection ability. Interestingly, even when a change was not detected, refixations on the changed object were longer than refixations on nonchanged objects. All of these results indicate that online representations do maintain information even in the absence of focused attention.

Hollingworth and Henderson (2002) expanded the demonstration that visual memory can be extracted and retained from a scene and proposed a model of the role of visual memory in scene representation. Similar to Hollingworth et al. (2001), participants were asked to view a scene for a later memory test, and while they viewed the scene, an object changed based on a saccade to a different object (again, there was a no-change control). As in Hollingworth et al., change-detection rates were not perfect, but above the false alarm rate. More critically, Hollingworth and Henderson found that participants could remember which version of the no-change control object (either token or rotation) that they saw even after several minutes. The ability to remember the object for minutes supports the critical role of memory in scene representations. Hollingworth and Henderson proposed that scene representations are supported by visual memory. Hollingworth (2005) extended the time between seeing a scene and testing change detection from immediate, to several minutes, to a full day after the scene had been seen. Even after a full day, the ability to detect the change was still above chance. Although visual memory is not perfect, it is sufficient to support token and rotation change detection under some conditions.

The findings of change blindness and good scene memory appear contradictory. How can they both exist in a single scene representation? There are several reasons that could work in concert in order to find both change blindness and retained visual memory for objects in a scene. One reason is related to the idea that central changes are easier to detect than marginal interest changes (Hollingworth & Henderson, 2002; Rensink et al., 1997). Detecting a change minimally requires that one fixate the object before it changes and after it changes; if there is no fixation on the object before it changes, there is effectively no change to detect. Objects of more central interest will likely be fixated earlier and thus increase the odds that a pre- and post-change fixation will take place (Hollingworth, 2005; Simons et al., 2002). While previous studies interpreted explicit change-detection failures as evidence of no visual memory (O'Regan, 1992; O'Regan et al., 1999; Rensink, 2000; Rensink et al., 1997), explicit change detection requires active comparison of the current perception with the former representation. Simons et al. (2002) probed the specific details that were changed in a real-life change-detection task. Although participants failed to notice the change when it occurred, they could recall the details of the changed object if specifically asked about it. The other aspect of the memory test for change detection is that explicit detection is a relatively high bar. Most researchers now believe that the change blindness does not arise from a lack of memory, but a combination of attention and memory processes (Intraub, 2010; Josephs et al., 2016; LaPointe et al., 2013).

Application in the Real World: Film Perception

As you sit in a theater, enjoying some popcorn and watching a movie, the number of processes required to understand the narrative, integrate visual and auditory information, and be sure to be looking at the right region at the right moment is impressive (Dorr et al., 2010; Hinde et al., 2017; Hutson et al., 2017; Loschky et al., 2015; Smith & Martin-Portugues Santacreu, 2017). Researchers have approached film perception in a variety of ways to provide some insight not only into how the processes happen, but also into the way in which movie-making techniques, developed over decades, fit with how we process information more generally. One example of this is in how cuts are made across scenes, which are referred to as Continuity Editing

Rules (Hecht & Kalkofen, 2009; Ildirar & Schwan, 2015; Magliano & Zacks, 2011; Smith & Henderson, 2008). With these rules, filmmakers have developed a number of different cuts to mask changes across scenes, minimize disruption to the narrative, and create a sense of timing, movement, and emotional responses (Anderson, 1996; Hecht & Kalkofen, 2009; Hinde et al., 2017; Loschky et al., 2015, 2020; Serrano et al., 2017; Smith & Henderson, 2008).

In one study, Smith and Henderson (2008) examined different types of cuts and measured participants' awareness of the cuts while their eye movements were monitored. Results showed that edits constructed in line with the Continuity Editing Rules result in less awareness of the edits than those that did not follow the rules. From the eye-movement record, the majority seem to be due to inattentional blindness, where the viewers are not aware of cuts because they are attending to the depicted narrative.

In another study, Smith et al. (2017) examined a specific type of editing called match-action. Match-action cuts attempt to create the impression of a continuous action by coinciding a cut with the onset of the action and showing that action in the subsequent shot (Anderson, 1996; Magliano & Zacks, 2011; Reisz & Millar, 1971). For example, in a match-action cut, the subject of the shot (e.g., a hand) is preserved across the edit and the action depicted continues across the shots (e.g., the hand reaches out and grabs an object across the cut). Editors believe that the continuation of motion makes the cut invisible (Murch, 2001). In their study, Smith et al. had participants perform a cut detection task while their eye movements were recorded and watched edits that manipulated the presence of motion before and after the critical match-action cut. In addition, the soundtrack was either included or was omitted. They found that removing post-cut motion (-post) or both pre-cut and post-cut motion (-both) significantly speeded up cut detection time and decreased the probability of missing the cut. In addition, they also found that cut detection time was significantly faster when clips were presented without audio. These results indicate that edit blindness may rely heavily on post-cut motion as well as the soundtrack to smooth processing of the narrative across cuts. Thus, across a number of recent studies it is clear that the evolution of editing rules that allow film viewers to easily follow a narrative goes hand in hand with research into understanding narratives and events, and leads to new insights into the processing of films as well as real-world events.

4 Long-Term Memory for Scenes

Although scene information can be extracted within the first 100 ms (Castelhano & Henderson, 2008b; Greene & Oliva, 2009b; Oliva, 2005; Potter, 1976), some of the representation is constructed over several fixations on the scene and then integrated with long-term memory of the scene. This stored representation can then be used to interpret the same or a similar scene in the future. As was discussed above, the percept of the world at any one point in time is that it is stable and detailed; this in turn has led many researchers to conclude that the visual representation formed for a scene is veridical and complete (Neisser & Kerr, 1973; Rayner & McConkie, 1976).

Early on, a number of studies showed how briefly viewed scenes could be recognized with high accuracy even when the scenes changed as it was too repetitive held in memory numbered in the thousands (Mandler & Johnson, 1976; Mandler & Ritchey, 1977; Nickerson, 1968; Shepard, 1967; Standing, 1973; Standing et al., 1970). This amazing feat of memory was thought to be possible only with highly detailed memory. In now classic memory studies, researchers demonstrated a high capacity for storing visual information about hundreds and even thousands of visual images (Nickerson, 1965, 1968; Shepard, 1967; Standing, 1973; Standing et al., 1970). These studies reveal that even with complex visual information, we are able to distinguish previously viewed scenes from novel ones at high performance levels (ranging from 92 percent to 98 percent) in a simple discrimination task. In one study, Standing et al. (1970) showed that when participants were asked to distinguish what had been previously viewed from the mirror-reversed versions of the same images, performance remained relatively high (88 percent). These researchers concluded that a considerable amount of detailed visual information is being stored in memory. Mandler and Ritchey (1977) examined the specific object information that was retained from a scene from 5 minutes to 4 months. Although recognition memory started to degrade when a week had passed, they found that information about the relative position of objects and what objects were (or were not) present was retained even up to 4 months. Other types of information like orientation, the exact spatial location, or the size of objects in the scene do not appear to be retained for as long.

Recent research has pointed to a resurgence in how detailed scene information is thought to be in long-term memory (Gronau & Shachar, 2015; Konkle et al., 2010; Summerfield et al., 2006). In one study, Konkle, Brady, Alvarez, and Oliva (2010) investigated the degree to which visual details of scenes are stored in visual long-term memory. They investigated whether object differences across images within scene categories would cause interference in memory performance. In their study, participants studied over 2,000 photographs from 128 different scene categories. For each scene category, the number of images presented during learning varied (from 1 to 64). The study replicated seminal studies on memory capacity for visual images with a high level of memory performance overall (96 percent), but accuracy decreased as more exemplars were present in a given category (84 percent to 76 percent from four to sixty-four categories, respectively). The decrease was relatively minor considering that for each doubling of exemplars, there was an approximately 2 percent decrease in memory accuracy. They concluded that for specific images within a category to be distinguished, a significant amount of visual detail must be stored. Based on these more recent studies, most researchers now posit that visual details such as the appearance of individual objects play a larger role in memory retrieval for scenes.

There has also been a great deal of research examining how scene details are encoded using the contextual cueing paradigm. The contextual cueing paradigm was first introduced by Chun and Jiang (1998), who found that participants were faster at finding letter targets in repeating arrays than in novel arrays. Brockmole, Castelhano, and Henderson (2006) extended this contextual cueing effect to real-world scenes and found similar results with faster performance when searching in a repeated scene. Furthermore, they found that compared to arrays, the effect was larger (~1–2 s) and learning occurred faster (within the first two to three blocks) with scenes. They concluded that the scene's semantic information played a key role in target location retrieval.

Brockmole, Castelhano, and Henderson (2006) examined whether the information being used to retrieve target location was based on the larger contextual (global) information or specific object (local) details (see Figure 8). They found that search performance was faster when the global, contextual information of a scene was repeated, compared to the local, object information. They concluded that targets in scenes were more strongly associated with a scene's global context compared to objects immediately surrounding the target. Brooks, Rasmussen, and Hollingworth (2010) further investigated how global scene information affected the encoding of local scene information. Brooks et al. proposed that targets are associated with a subregion of the scene. They found that a functional subregion can be associated with a global context during learning, and the global context can be used later to find the subregion and target. However, if the global context was not paired with the subregion and target during learning, then the scene–target association was not learned independently of the subregion.

Based on their findings, Brooks et al. (2010) suggested a hierarchical model of scene representations in long-term memory. In this model, a global context can be broken down into nested subregions. The model is based on a series of navigation studies that demonstrated that memory for larger environments is organized hierarchically (Hirtle & Jonides, 1985; McNamara, 1986; McNamara

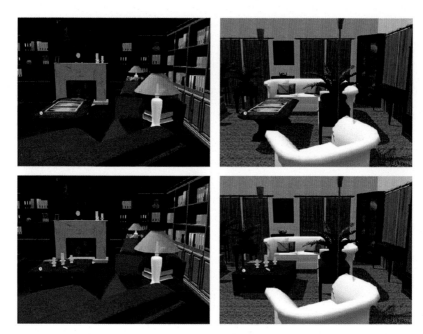

Figure 8 Example images in which the local details were changed (coffee table) or the global details were changed (room). See text for details. Taken with permission from Brockmole et al. (2006).

et al., 1989). These navigation studies examined memory for spatial relations in subregions of a larger environment. The subregions were distinct clusters defined by their content objects and were also nested within the larger environment. They found that navigation and recall of the details of the subregions depended on the observer's ability to retrieve information about the larger environment. Concerning scenes, the application of such a model would mean that the retrieval of information in any one part of the scene (e.g., contents on a desk) would depend on the recognition of the background or larger contextual information (e.g., a specific office).

In a more recent study, Castelhano, Fernandes, and Theriault (2018) examined whether accessing the scene context was needed to access more specific scene information in a hierarchical manner. To do so, they used chimera scenes, which were scene images in which the background and foreground came from different scene categories (see Figure 9). They found that when the information immediately surrounding the target was changed, the contextual cueing effect was not completely abolished; some information about the target location was retrievable from the background context information. Similar to previous studies (Brockmole et al., 2006; Brockmole & Henderson, 2006), when the

Figure 9 Example stimuli used in the Castelhano et al. (2018) study. On the left-hand side, the original normal scenes are shown. These have their foregrounds switched to produce the chimera scenes, shown on the right-hand side.

surrounding background information was changed (global change transfer condition), they found a similarly decreased, but not altogether abolished, contextual cueing effect. The finding that a changed background can permit some retrieval of the target information indicates that not all information about the target is routed through information about the larger scene context in a strictly hierarchical manner.

Another aspect of a scene that can be retained and used in subsequent processing is the scene's spatial layout. The layout of the scene is specific to the image that one is viewing, as one can imagine that the same space can be viewed from different perspectives (see Figure 10). The spatial layout can directly inform the scene representation across viewpoints. For instance, Sanocki and Epstein (1997) found that the scene layout information prime could be used in a subsequent judgment of a matching scene, specifically depth information. However, when the scene prime was different, performance was no better than a no-scene-control preview, indicating a boost from the same layout but no cost arising from having processed a different layout. In subsequent studies, researchers have shown that scene layout can be extrapolated to some extent beyond the current view (Castelhano, Pollatsek, et al., 2009;

Figure 10 The same space depicted from different viewpoints and conveying different aspects of the spatial layout. See text for details.

Castelhano & Pollatsek, 2010; Gottesman, 2011; Sanocki, 2003; Sanocki & Epstein, 1997). For instance, Castelhano and Pollatsek (2010) had participants indicate which of two dots superimposed on a scene image appeared closer to them in depth. They found that when the priming scene was identical or only 10° (rotated to the right or left), priming of depth occurred, but there was no reliable priming from larger differences in viewpoint (20° or greater). However, it should be noted that not all researchers accept that scene layout can be reliably extrapolated from a current view. Shafer-Skelton and Brady (2019) argued that the priming found in Sanocki and Epstein's study did not arise from scene layout, but rather was the result of iconic memory match between the prime and target scenes. When a 200-ms dynamic mask was presented between the prime and the target scene, they found the spatial layout priming disappeared. However, this is still debated as it is not yet clear what the presence of a dynamic mask would do to the representation and how it would affect subsequent processing, regardless of the processing type (spatial or otherwise).

In addition to more general properties like gist and spatial layout, the particular objects that appear in the scene also affect the retention of scenes in long-term memory. The extraction of object information is not as rapid as the extraction of global scene information and tends to build up over time (Hollingworth, 2004). Importantly, when moving their eyes around the scene, people do not look at wide, homogenous expanses of the scene (e.g., the sky).

Instead, they look at the objects that occur in the scene. As people look around the scene, they are extracting object representations that can be integrated into the scene's representation. To study the long-term representation of scenes and the relation of the objects contained within them, Hollingworth (2004) examined visual memory for objects in scenes using a follow-the-dot paradigm to ensure that objects were fixated and in a specific order. After looking at the scene and the objects, one of the objects in the sequence was tested. The most recently viewed objects were remembered best, highlighting a role of visual working memory, but Hollingworth found that even objects viewed in the more distant past were remembered well.

It is important to note how the retention of information in long-term memory was first thought to be highly detailed, then thought to be quite sparse, and is now thought to be somewhere in between. Nonetheless, the notion that there is no memory for visual information is no longer held to be true. Based on more recent findings, it may be that the retention of information may depend more on what is noticed and recalled during retrieval processes, rather than the amount of information that is retained. Across studies, many researchers now believe it may be that more details are encoded than there are details recalled.

In addition, researchers have examined how well objects are remembered across the visual field. In an early study, Parker (1978) claimed that object information could be extracted far into the periphery, allowing people to move their eyes to objects that changed if that was needed. In contrast, Henderson et al. (2003) found that to detect changes to objects, one had to be within 4° of visual angle to detect the change in a complex scene (in this case, three-dimensional renderings of real-world scenes). In a more recent study, Pereira and Castelhano (2014) found that object information interacted with the peripheral scene information when guiding the eyes to a target. If objects around the target were present in the periphery, the eyes were more likely to move to that area, indicating that people select object-filled areas to look at when looking for a target object. There is a preference to look toward object clusters. Together, these studies suggest that objects are a unit of memory as well as a unit of attentional guidance, which we will examine further below.

Application in the Real World: False Memory

Even now, with the ubiquitous nature of photos on devices and in social media, photographs are powerful sources of influence on memory. When examining photographs of a past event, they often act as a memory cue to recall the events of a specific day and time. In the past, photographs were seen as a reliable and undisputed memory cue, even as our own memories are considerably more unreliable (Dodhia & Metcalfe, 1999; Garry & Gerrie, 2005; Lindsay et al., 2004; Liv & Greenbaum, 2020; Wade et al., 2002). In fact, many studies examining the malleability of memories have used photographs to examine how autobiographical memories are affected (Garry & Gerrie, 2005; Garry & Wade, 2005; Lindsay et al., 2004; Wade et al., 2002). Many studies found that even when there was no evidence that a person had experienced a specific event in their life, providing a photograph as a potential cue led many individuals to falsely report the event. For instance, Wade and colleagues (2002) had participants recall three events from their childhood, two of which were real (gathered through interviews with their parents) and one that was false (e.g., a hot air balloon ride). The manipulation included a narrative of the false memory, a photograph, and imagery instructions. The photograph was doctored to include the participant and a parent in a hot air balloon. With this manipulation, they were able to create false childhood memories in 35 percent of the participants. Further, they examined the details in the recall using a clause analysis to explore the extent to which the fake photograph had contributed to the false memory. They found that the details of the photograph made up on average about 30 percent of the participants' clauses in the description of the event, but false memories were more likely than true memories to contain detail from the photograph. Thus, they concluded that the photograph did act to support details in the false memory and increase the believability of the story for some participants.

Since the Wade et al. (2002) study, many other researchers have investigated the effects of photographs on the memory of events (Cardwell et al., 2016; Liv & Greenbaum, 2020; Nash, 2018; Newman et al., 2020). Researchers have found that the memory of events was malleable even when the event was general public knowledge. In one such study, Nash (2018) manipulated photos from two public events (the 2012 London Olympic torch relay and the 2011 royal wedding of Prince William and Kate Middleton). Photos depicted the real-life events as they occurred or were doctored to include protesters and violence. Nash also manipulated whether the doctoring of the photos was high or low quality and added disclaimers that would warn about their inauthenticity. Despite all the potential warnings about the manipulations, he found that some participants were still more likely to believe in the unrest at these events when they were accompanied by a photo, regardless of the quality of the changes or the presence of the disclaimer. Nash concluded that the photos seem to add credibility to the story, even when other measures were taken to warn participants to discount them. This addition of photos, even when they have no bearing on the event itself, has been supported in other studies (Cardwell et al., 2016; Henkel & Milliken, 2020; Newman et al., 2020). Thus, it seems that photographs play an important role in changing people's perception of a public event and convey a sense of credibility, even when unwarranted.

Traditionally, memory susceptibility to suggestion and change was researched in the context of eyewitness memory (for a review, see Loftus, 2019), where many researchers found that subsequent retelling of an event had a marked influence on how that event was subsequently recalled. However, in more recent years, more attention has been directed toward people's susceptibility to believing fake news stories (Murphy et al., 2019; Pennycook & Rand, 2019; Spinney, 2017). For instance, Murphy et al. (2019) had participants view six news stories (two fake) after Ireland's abortion referendum and manipulated the photos to coincide with partici-pants' political stance or against it. They found that almost half the partici-pants reported remembering the fake news story, and a third of those remembered specific details about the event. A subsequent analysis showed that the believability depended on the participants' political orientation, with greater memory for fake stories about a scandal on the opposing side.

Despite all the studies suggesting that memory of events and memory of photos may play an important role, there remain quite a few researchers that have argued that these studies are misleading and may not have any direct bearing on the existence and believability of fake news (Liv & Greenbaum, 2020; Nichols & Loftus, 2019; Patihis et al., 2018). Instead, some researchers have argued that the experiments are set up in such a way as to coerce participants to behave or answer in certain ways that align with the researchers' expectations (demand characteristics of the experiments result in higher rates of believing fake news). Interestingly, photographs as a memory cue are used both to suggest that the fake story is true and as a way to cue more accurate information to offset the false information. For instance, Smelter and Calvillo (2020) found that the mere presence of a photograph with a headline increased its perceived accuracy regardless of whether the headline was true or false. We expect much more focus in the future on the consumption and prevention of fake news and its relation to false memories.

5 Eye Movements and Scenes

In this section, we will focus on the use of eye movements to examine how scenes are processed and understood. Although eye movements provide an excellent record of the location and timing of the eyes, their usefulness arises from their connection to mental processes. The structure of the eye forces us naturally to move them as it is only from the central point of gaze that we have the highest acuity (the fovea, ~2° of visual angle; see Figure 11). To compensate for this limited area of high acuity, people rotate their eyes in order to extract highly detailed visual information from areas of interest. We do so automatically and most people are unaware that the eyes move a number of times per second (~ 3 eye movements per second: Rayner, 2009; Williams & Castelhano, 2019). Although not always implicit, the ease with which we move our eyes and the relative "invisibility" of these movements make them an ideal tool for observing behavioral responses unobtrusively (Castelhano et al., 2007; Rayner, 2009; Williams & Castelhano, 2019).

Some of the earliest demonstrations of eye-movement patterns showed that they reflected different ways in which information was processed (Buswell, 1935; Yarbus, 1967). Buswell and Yarbus both described the importance of the task that the observer is performing. Buswell (1935) demonstrated that when participants were told to view the pictures in a "normal manner," he found that the fixation were widespread. When the tasks had less focused instructions, participants had a greater tendency to scan a large proportion of the scene as there remains uncertainty of the importance of any particular detail. However, when participants searched for a person in a window in the same scene that they had freely viewed previously, the fixations were concentrated on possible locations where the target could be. In other words, when given specific instructions in a task, such as a target object to search for, eye movements tend to be focused on possible scene areas in which that

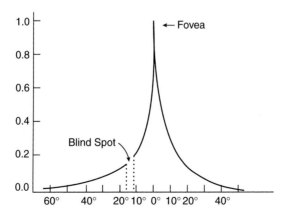

Figure 11 Highest acuity corresponds with the center of vision, which is lined up with the fovea in the retina. Acuity rapidly declines outside this area with increased eccentricity from the fovea. Based on Rayner and Castelhano (2007a).

object can occur. Similarly, Yarbus (1967) examined the eye movements of a participant when looking at a single stimulus, the painting *An Unexpected Visitor*, with different tasks. Yarbus found that the locations of fixations varied with the task (see also DeAngelus & Pelz, 2009), demonstrating that the task performed can alter the eye-movement patterns dramatically as different aspects of the scene are relevant to each task. The studies of both Buswell and Yarbus highlighted the usefulness of the eye-movement record for deciphering cognitive processes.

Since these early studies, researchers have further investigated how different eye-movement measures reflect cognitive processing and attention (Castelhano, Mack, et al., 2009; Castelhano & Henderson, 2007; Castelhano & Krzyś, 2020; Castelhano & Pereira, 2018; Castelhano & Rayner, 2008; Deubel & Schneider, 1996; Hoffman & Subramaniam, 1995; Rayner et al., 1978; Williams & Castelhano, 2019). While the early studies described results as qualitative differences observed in the eye-movement record, more modern methods examine eye movements in terms of the time spent and spatial distribution of the record. Saccadic eye movements rotate the eyes from pointing at one part of the visual world to another and generally take less than 50 ms (Awh et al., 2006; Rayner, 2009; Reichle et al., 1998; Williams & Castelhano, 2019). Once the eyes have rotated to point to the new location, they pause or fixate for a brief amount of time (e.g., 100–400 ms). While the eye is in motion, visual processing from the eyes is limited through saccadic suppression and no visual information is acquired (Deubel et al., 2002; Rayner, 2009). Thus, for the purpose of examining cognitive processing, the point at which the eye is relatively still (such as during a fixation) is of greatest interest.

The eye-movement measures used to examine scene processing have borrowed greatly from the reading literature and reflect different fixation measures based on duration, number/count, and location. However, aggregate fixation measures that define processing across different temporal windows have proven to be especially useful. For instance, gaze duration (the sum of the fixation durations on a region of interest from the first fixation in the region to when the eyes leave that region) can give an indication of the time to initially process and recognize an object. Subsequent fixations (second gaze duration or total time) also indicate additional information gathering was needed or that a checking/confirming process was necessary.

In contrast to these measures based on reading, researchers are also interested in the spatial distribution of fixations in scenes. The spatially distributed information of eye movements allows researchers to have a direct measure of prioritization of information available to the observer, examine commonalities in the prioritization across individuals, and allow for other interesting spatially aggregate measures. For instance, the proportion of the image fixated can indicate the extent of the exploratory vs. focused behavior. Some tasks encourage greater exploration of the scene (e.g., memorization), whereas others constrain that exploration (e.g., visual search). Further to this, scan path ratio is a measure that indicates the degree of efficiency of the eye movements as it can be used to create a ratio of the distance taken to reach a critical region to the shortest distance possible. Thus, with all 360° of possible locations of the next fixation, the spatial dimension allows for a rich set of measures that reflect different types of processing.

In addition to the spatial dimension, because the eyes move from one location to the next in a serial manner, eye-movement data provide a temporal record of processing. This information allows researchers to identify the order in which scene features are processed, indicating their relative importance to the task. In addition, fixations typically last only a few hundred milliseconds, which is much shorter than many complex tasks (e.g., searching) take to complete. The serial fixation record can be examined to determine, at a more fine-grained time scale, the processing that was occurring at each point in the trial rather than on a global scale (i.e., reaction time).

The timing and placement of eye movements is an important measure of cognitive processing only because eye movements are strongly linked to attentional processes. Research has found that when the eyes move, attention precedes the eyes to the intended location and remains at that location for some time before moving to another location (Castelhano & Pereira, 2018; Gordon et al., 2008; Rayner, 2009; Zelinsky, 2008). Although not absolute (attention can move to locations independently of the eyes), fixation location is linked to the attended regions of the visual stimuli. We turn to this connection next.

5.1 Eye Movements and Attention

Over the past few decades, researchers have established that there is a tight link between eye movements and attention (Casarotti et al., 2012; Cavanagh et al., 2010; Rolfs et al., 2011; Zhao et al., 2012). In a seminal study, Hoffman and Subramaniam (1995) demonstrated that attending to one location while saccading to another did not improve performance at the attended location, but instead improvement was seen at the location of the saccade landing point. From this, researchers have demonstrated not only that attention is tightly linked with the planning and execution of an eye movement to a new location, but also that it presents an interesting conundrum for interpreting fixation durations. As stated earlier, the decision of where to move the eye is inherently a part of measures reflecting when to move the eyes. Thus, the link between eye movement and attentional processes is not a straightforward causal relationship as posited by a number of early studies (e.g., Rizzolatti et al., 1987). Recent studies do not dispute the link between attention and eye movements, but rather highlight how information processing at different positions relative to the current eye position is updated over time and introduces a more fractured view of the role of attention relative to eye movements.

For instance, in a recent study Castelhano and Pereira (2018) examined the contribution of the global semantic context to the planning and execution of a fixation to a critical object. To do so, they used a modified version of a boundary paradigm (Rayner, 1975; Rayner et al., 2009a, 2010), called the dot boundary paradigm (see Figure 12). In the original paradigm, when a participant's fixation crossed an invisible boundary, a critical word changed from a preview word to the target word. They could be orthographically or semantically related, and fixation on the target word showed how much of the preview word was processed prior to direct fixation. In the modified dot boundary paradigm, participants are asked to first fixate on a red circle that suddenly appeared on the scene image. This allowed for the information from the preview object to be controlled as it appeared within a certain distance from that circle. Following fixation on the red circle, a preview object would suddenly appear, which would capture attention (Brockmole & Henderson, 2005; Pannasch & Velichkovsky, 2009). The participants' task was to verify the identity of this critical object (Castelhano & Pereira, 2018). Once a saccade toward the preview object was made and an invisible boundary that surrounded the target object was crossed, the preview object changed to the target object. Fixation patterns on the target object revealed how much information had been extracted and processed prior to fixation. The results showed that information extracted from the object prior to fixation was influenced by the overall semantic consistency between it and the scene context. This effect was seen in early measures of fixating on the target object, but not on later measures or aggregate measures of eye movements.

Other influences on the direction of attention and eye movements have recently come to the fore. For instance, idiosyncratic eye-movement tendencies for how information is acquired have an additional effect on guidance (Bindemann, 2010; Castelhano & Henderson, 2008a; Castelhano & Rayner, 2008; Tatler, 2007; Tseng et al., 2009). For instance, there is the central bias effect (Tatler, 2007), where the eyes have a bias to look to the center of the image. While initial eye movements seem to be positioned centrally, this effect dissipates with time (Bindemann, 2010; Rothkegel et al., 2017). In addition to

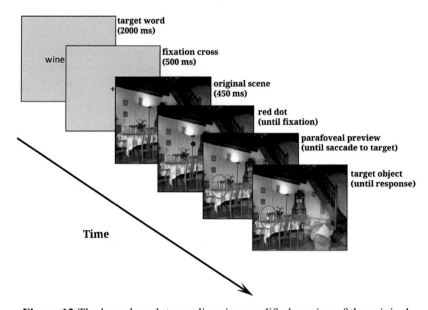

Figure 12 The boundary dot paradigm is a modified version of the original boundary paradigm used in reading to account for the varied direction of saccades during scene viewing. In the dot paradigm, the participants were first shown the target word, followed by a fixation cross and an initial viewing of the scene image (presented without the target or the preview object). After 450 ms of viewing, a red dot appeared, and participants were instructed to fixate on the dot. Once fixated, the preview object would onset (highlighted here for illustrative purposes, although the participants would not see the object highlighted). Participants were instructed to verify whether this object was the target object and during a saccade toward that object, the preview would change to the target object. Taken with permission from Castelhano and Pereira (2018). See text for more details.

a central bias effect, Bindeman (2010) found that the screen size and boundaries play a role as only early eye movements were directed to the center.

In addition to global eye-movement tendencies, people also have individual differences in their tendencies in the execution of fixations and saccades (Castelhano & Henderson, 2008a; Rayner et al., 2007). Castelhano and Henderson (2008a) revealed that there were individual tendencies both in the length of fixations and saccades. They found that individuals had tendencies toward shorter or longer fixations and shorter or longer saccades. Interestingly, there was no relationship between tendencies between fixation and saccade lengths, such that a shorter "fixater" could equally be a longer or shorter "saccader." These individual tendencies have also been linked to how well regions of interest are processed and how these change across individuals in special populations (e.g., individuals with Autism Spectrum Disorders; Au-Yeung et al., 2011; Benson et al., 2012; Benson et al., 2016; Williams & Castelhano, 2019). Although it is outside the scope of the current review, many recent studies have used eye movement to examine individual differences across a number of special populations. Thus, across both global and individual tendencies, internal biases also have an influence on how fixation patterns emerge in any given situation. However, rather than focusing on internal influences on eye movements, much of the research on eye-movement guidance has been focused on external influences.

5.2 Scene Properties and Eye-Movement Guidance

Traditionally, researchers have examined how image features drive eye movements in a bottom-up manner. Computer vision has been incredibly influential in how researchers theorize how eye movements are guided, most predominantly through computational models of saliency (Itti et al., 1998; Itti & Koch, 2000). Visual saliency and saliency maps try to define areas that "stand out" from the background as potential points of interest (Henderson et al., 2007). When looking at images, the eyes rarely go to large homogenous areas such as a blue sky or a blank wall (Buswell, 1935; Mackworth & Morandi, 1967; Yarbus, 1967). Saliency calculations attempt to find the areas of the image based on the low-level features that can be extracted from the image itself. Saliency maps highlight the coordinates of the points that stand out and allow for a ranking of importance within the image. Low-level features such as color, orientation, and intensity (Borji et al., 2013; Itti & Koch, 2000), as well as second-order features such as intersections and edges (Erdem & Erdem, 2013; Frey et al., 2007), have been found to affect eye-movement planning. Although many researchers have explored the combined and separate contributions of low-level features to eye-movement guidance (such as color: Nuthmann & Malcolm, 2016), there has been movement away from a purely bottom-up approach.

Although saliency has inspired a number of theoretical models and research studies, over the past decade the limits of saliency as an explanatory tool have become more pronounced (Bruce et al., 2015; Henderson et al., 2007; Latif et al., 2014; Tatler et al., 2011). First, inherent in models of saliency is the notion that information selection is passive and based solely on the properties of the image, regardless of the individual's intent. For instance, Latif et al. (2014) found that when examining different versions of the painting *The Death of General Wolfe* by Benjamin West, fixations were drawn to different areas of the painting depending on their saliency. Notably, when the saliency of the two versions of the painting was modified such that each was changed to the other's saliency patterns (making the high-saliency area low and vice versa), participants showed eye-movement patterns that corresponded to the changed saliency of the painting, leading authors to conclude that when directed to look at the painting to understand the event depicted, the saliency of different regions affects the pattern and distribution of eye movements. However, across many studies, it should be noted that individuals are actively seeking visual input, regardless of the task (Castelhano, Mack, et al., 2009; Tatler et al., 2011).

Second, there is an overall movement away from classifying influences as either purely top-down or bottom-up (Awh et al., 2012; Tatler et al., 2011). Instead, researchers have begun to examine different sources of information (e.g., immediate history with a task) and how they are combined and interact. For instance, many recent models are finding ways to incorporate higher-level information such as meaning and objects into how scene information is selected (Kanan et al., 2009; Zelinsky, 2008). There are many computational models that have since been proposed to better represent higher-order information, but review of that work is beyond the scope of the current Element (see Zelinsky et al., 2020, for a review). However, we will consider the different types of higher-order information and their influence on eye-movement guidance.

5.3 Influence of Semantics on Eye Movements

The effect of higher-order influences has received greater attention in the last decade as researchers move away from solely examining low-level, stimulus properties as the main influence on eye-movement guidance. The influence of scene semantics on eye-movement guidance is usually investigated by comparing semantic consistent details with inconsistent ones within a larger context. Any differences in fixating on consistent and inconsistent objects are attributed to scene semantics because inconsistency is defined by the object–scene relationship. Although semantic inconsistency can influence eye movements in multiple ways (Benson et al., 2012, 2016; Castelhano & Heaven, 2011; Castelhano & Rayner, 2008; Rayner et al., 2009b), researchers have concentrated on two main questions: (1) whether inconsistent objects capture attention from a distance and (2) how inconsistency affects object processing and recognition. We examine each in turn.

How and whether semantic inconsistencies can be identified in the periphery and then attract attention has been debated for a number of decades. In a now seminal study, Loftus and Mackworth (1978) found that a semantically inconsistent object (e.g., an octopus in a farmyard) was more likely to be fixated on than a consistent object (e.g., a tractor in a farmyard) and, importantly, was fixated on sooner. They concluded that the inconsistent semantic objects automatically attract attention. Despite being intuitively appealing, subsequent studies produced mixed results (Becker et al., 2007; De Graef et al., 1990; Henderson et al., 1999; Underwood et al., 2007), and this inconsistency has also been found in more recent studies (Castelhano & Heaven, 2010, 2011; LaPointe & Milliken, 2016; Võ & Henderson, 2009, 2011). For instance, Castelhano and Heaven (2011) found that objects that were inconsistent with the scene context (e.g., cookbook in a bathroom) did not attract fixations sooner and, in fact, often took longer to attract fixations than consistent objects. These findings suggest that attention was not immediately drawn to semantically inconsistent objects.

In contrast to the original study by Loftus and Mackworth (1978), studies in the past decade have found that consistent objects lead to more efficient search performance (Castelhano & Heaven, 2010, 2011; Hwang et al., 2011; Malcolm & Henderson, 2009; Pereira & Castelhano, 2014). Researchers posit that the semantic relatedness of the object not only to the scene context but also to other objects in the scenes led to faster search. For instance, Hwang et al. (2011) used annotated photo images (from LabelMe Database; Russell et al., 2008) to examine the contribution of semantically related objects to the guidance of eye movements. They found that there was a tendency for the next fixation to be programmed to an object that was semantically similar to the currently fixated object. Further, Mack and Eckstein (2011) found that when semantically related objects were placed in close proximity, search was much faster. On the other hand, Lapointe and Milliken (2016) found inconsistent objects were detected more quickly during a change-detection task. The difference in patterns of results illustrates important interactions between stimulus properties (e.g., the size of the critical object) and task (e.g., visual search vs. change detection), and so the influence of semantics on eye-movement guidance is more nuanced than a simple yes or no.

Second, researchers have also examined the question of how semantic inconsistencies affect object recognition processing once they are fixated. This question is less contentious as it has been well established that inconsistent objects do lead to overall longer processing times (De Graef et al., 1990; Friedman, 1979; Henderson et al., 1999). For example, Friedman (1979) found that objects that were inconsistent with the scene's semantic category led to longer fixation durations and the increase in fixation duration was in line with the degree of inconsistency of the object within that scene according to the ratings by a separate group of participants (varied from high to low inconsistency).

More recent studies have demonstrated similar results (Castelhano & Heaven, 2010, 2011; Malcolm & Henderson, 2009; Võ & Wolfe, 2013a). However, in addition, there are some differences in where objects are placed within the inconsistent scene. Castelhano and Heaven (2011) had participants search for objects placed in an inconsistent scene context that were either in a consistent region of the scene (e.g., cookbook on a bathroom countertop) or in an inconsistent region in the scene (e.g., on the floor of the bathroom). An example of the stimuli manipulation is shown in Figure 13. They found that when processing the object, the placement of the object within the larger scene context had an effect on object recognition processes such that inconsistent placement in an inconsistent context led to longer fixation durations than the consistent placement. It is not completely clear why this would be the case, as in each case the semantic mismatch remains. However, work on the parsing of the object from the background (Oliva & Torralba, 2007) reveals that an object placed within an expected location may be easier to parse, but more research is needed to draw a more definitive conclusion.

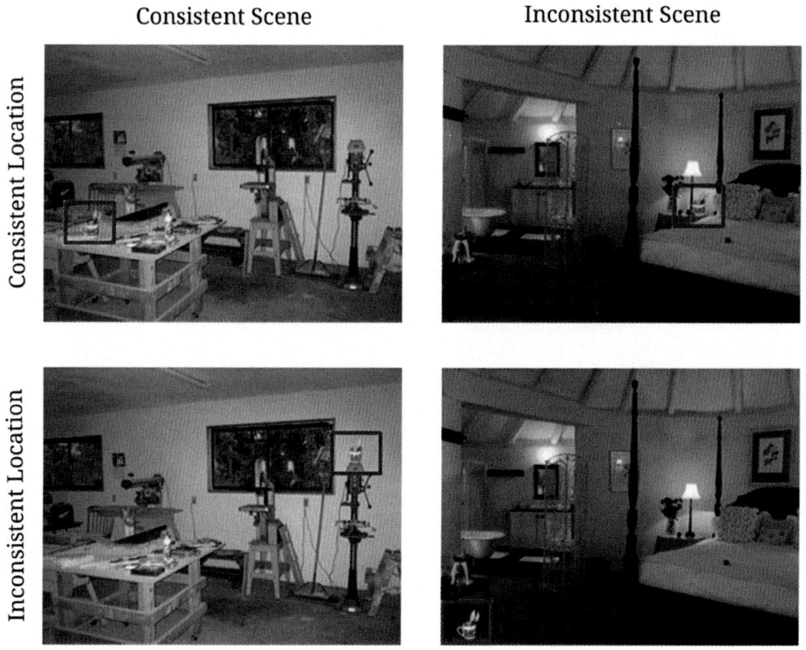

Figure 13 The stimuli used in the Castelhano and Heaven (2011) study manipulated the placement of the target objects such that both the semantic consistency and spatial placement were manipulated orthogonally. Taken with permission from Castelhano and Heaven (2011). See text for more details.

5.4 Influence of Task and Intention on Eye Movements

Looking again to the work of Buswell (1935) and Yarbus (1967), it is easily seen how the task being performed is critical when interpreting eye movements and scene processing. Since then and with the rapid development of eye-movement tracking technology, researchers have used eye movements to examine the cognitive underpinnings of processing across a number of tasks. In addition, with improvements in the tracking technology, researchers have sought to determine how task affects eye-movement patterns quantitatively (Castelhano, Mack, et al., 2009; Greene & Wolfe, 2011; Haji-Abolhassani & Clark, 2014; Henderson et al., 2013; Land & Hayhoe, 2001; Mills et al., 2011; Tatler et al., 2011; Triesch et al., 2003). For example, Castelhano et al. (2009) examined eye-movement patterns across visual search and memorization tasks on the same set of stimuli. Participants first completed one task and then another, and the pictures were counterbalanced across participants. This design allowed for a direct comparison of the effect of the task while having the differences in stimuli consistent. They found that the dispersion of fixations across the stimuli differed, in that fixations were more widely dispersed in the memorization task than in the visual search task. In addition, they found that while individual fixation durations were task invariant, task differences arose in the aggregate measure of fixations. So, while the individual fixation durations remained the same across tasks, the task affected how many times the same region of the scene was re-fixated on. Interestingly, some researchers have also found task differences at the level of the individual fixation, in addition to the aggregate measures (Nuthmann, 2017). From these results, it is important to note the task differences in motivation and strategy that influence how a scene is fixated on and processed.

The contrast between memorization and visual search tasks used in Castelhano et al. (2009) demonstrates differences between a wide variety of tasks. Notably, the extent to which fixations are dispersed across a scene is tied to how restrictive the instructions are. Many times, tasks that minimally direct the participant are used, such as memorization (Castelhano, Mack, et al., 2009; Cronin et al., 2020; Henderson & Castelhano, 2005; Williams & Castelhano, 2019; Zelinsky & Loschky, 2005), aesthetic judgments (Choe et al., 2017; Heidenreich & Turano, 2011; Hristova et al., 2011; Rosenberg & Klein, 2015), and free viewing (Hristova et al., 2011; Latif et al., 2014; Mills et al., 2011; Nuthmann, 2017). These less focused tasks encourage participants to scan a large proportion of the scene as participants are uncertain of the importance of any particular detail. However, this breadth is not of uniform density and tends to be focused on parts of the scenes where meaningful objects exist (Antes, 1974; Castelhano, Mack, et al., 2009; Castelhano & Krzyś, 2020; Castelhano &

Rayner, 2008; Henderson & Hayes, 2017; Mackworth & Morandi, 1967; Williams & Castelhano, 2019). Thus, less focused instructions also lead to less focused eye-movement patterns.

In contrast, highly focused tasks, like visual search, require participants to be more directed in their viewing in line with a specific goal. In an early example of this contrast, Buswell (1935) demonstrated that when participants searched for a person in a window in the same scene that they had freely viewed previously, fixations were concentrated on the windows of the building, or the possible locations of the target. In general, the extent of the eye movements executed under search instructions tends to be more focused on areas of the scene in which the object is likely to occur (Castelhano & Krzyś, 2020; Oliva et al., 2003; Pereira & Castelhano, 2019; Torralba et al., 2006).

Because a search task necessitates that some scene regions are relevant and some are not, they allow researchers to investigate the way attention is allocated by manipulating the relative importance of other properties of the scene. For example, Pereira and Castelhano (2019) had participants search for a target object while on half the trials an unexpected distractor object could suddenly appear. The distractor object could appear either in a relevant scene region (corresponding to a scene region likely to contain the target object) or an irrelevant region (in which the target would be unlikely to be located) (see Figure 14). They found that attention was more likely to be captured by the distractor appearing in the relevant region than the irrelevant region. When participants searched for a letter target, which had no association with any scene context region, there was no difference in attentional capture across regions. Based on this pattern of results, they concluded that the allocation of attention was focused on the region of the scene most relevant to the search task target. The differences in patterns between tasks led researchers to examine how else eye movements could shed light on the type of processing being conducted at the time.

Application in the Real World: Marketing and Ads

Based on the work examining how attention is directed within real-world environments, tools have been developed to examine how attention to advertisements is processed and, in turn, how effective different types of marketing strategies are. Within this field of research, eye movements have become an important tool; for example, research on eye movements has been linked to research on marketing and processing of ads (Aribarg & Schwartz, 2020; Bassett-Gunter et al., 2014; Hervet et al., 2011; Pieters & Wedel, 2004;

Object Search   Letter Search

Figure 14 An example of the stimuli used in the Pereira and Castelhano (2019) study on the deployment of attention in scenes during visual search (target object highlighted in blue). The paradigm used the sudden onset of a distractor object (highlighted in red). The distractor occurred in either a target-consistent scene region or in an inconsistent one. As a control, measures of distraction were also taken when searching for a letter target, which has no contextual constraints. Taken with permission from Pereira and Castelhano (2019). See text for details.

Rayner et al., 2001, 2008; Rayner & Castelhano, 2007b; van der Lans & Wedel, 2017; Wedel, 2017; Wedel & Pieters, 2000).

Prior to the late 1990s, most of the research on eye movements of viewers examining print advertisements tended to be descriptive (see Radach et al., 2003 for a summary). More recent research has focused on attempts to quantitatively determine how different aspects of the ad and the viewer's goal interact to affect gaze patterns to different parts of the ad. For example, Rayner et al. (2001) asked participants (from the United States) to imagine that they had just moved to the United Kingdom and that they needed to either buy a new car (the car condition) or skin care products (the skin care condition). Both groups of participants saw the same set of unfamiliar ads. In the car group, participants saw eight critical car ads, but they also saw eight critical skin car ads and eight filler ads (consisting of a variety of ad types); participants in the skin care group saw the same ads. With this setup, the two different types of ads have different levels of relevance to each of the groups. Perhaps unsurprisingly, they found the car group spent more time looking at car ads than at skin care ads, while the skin care group spent more time looking at skin care ads than car ads. In a follow-up study, Rayner et al. (2008) had participants rate the ad in terms of (1) its effectiveness and (2) how likeable it was. Interestingly, the gaze patterns of this study were different from the earlier Rayner et al. (2001) study. In Rayner et al. (2008), when asked to rate pictures for effectiveness or likeability, participants tended to spend more time looking at the picture in the ad compared to its text. In contrast, participants in the Rayner et al. (2001) study spent more time reading the text, particularly if the ad was relevant to their task. Thus, when the task was to buy a product, participants spent more time reading; when the task was to rate the ad, they spent more time examining the picture.

Although studies examining viewing of advertisement directly have revealed different patterns of engagement with each part, other research studies have examined how advertisements are viewed in the context of other material (example content from a news outlet, social media, etc.). Positioning ads around the edges of the screen has led viewers to develop what researchers term "banner blindness" (Hervet et al., 2011; Margarida Barreto, 2013; Resnick & Albert, 2014). Banner blindness was a term coined to refer to the tendency for viewers to ignore information presented in certain formats or in certain positions within a webpage (Benway & Lane, 1998). For instance, Resnick and Albert (2014) found that banner blindness was most often exhibited in cases in which participants were given a specific task and when the ad took up the upper-right location in the screen. This was most often revealed as a complete lack of engagement with the advertisement (no direct looks to the ad and a lack of memory for either the ad or the brand being advertised). Researchers have concluded that because advertisements are made in such a way that they attempt to grab attention (often colorful and with motion or depicting movement), viewers learn the typical features of online ads and learn to ignore and avoid them. This finding has led to the development of alternative means of advertising online, which we turn to next.

More recently, researchers have examined how different approaches to online advertising affect attention to and processing of advertisements. Native advertising is a type of advertising where the ad is placed in-feed and its form and format matches the context of the platform on which it is displayed (e.g., ads on Facebook or Instagram as formatted to appear as content of the feed). This is thought to be more effective than advertisements that are placed in specific locations on the display (Aribarg & Schwartz, 2020; Hervet et al., 2011; Higgins et al., 2014; Margarida Barreto, 2013; Resnick & Albert, 2014) because the same feature cues are not as readily available to viewers. In fact, many early studies found that the content of the advertisements was often taken as content itself, speaking to its effectiveness in having people engage with the ads. In a recent study, Aribarg and Schwartz (2020) had participants view either display or native advertisements while viewing a news webpage. They examined the ads' effectiveness for brand recognition and clickthrough rate as well as eye-movement patterns as measures of engagement. They found certain tradeoffs between the two that did not clearly elevate one format as superior to the other. Eye-movement patterns revealed a greater amount of time looking at display ads than native ads as well as better explicit memory for the display ads. However, they also found a greater rate of clicks for the native ads than display ads. These results present an interesting conundrum: because different measures reveal different patterns of engagement, the main question becomes: which type is most desirable? Although banner blindness is a widely accepted notion, advertising strategies that try to circumvent these particular issues have shown varying degrees of success, depending on which measure is used. Nonetheless, eye-movement patterns do reveal an interesting contrast between how viewers process information once it is fixated and whether they want to delve into it more.

Although advertisements differ in a variety of ways, there are some under-lying principles in how viewers inspect them. First, when viewers look at an ad with the expectation that they might want to buy a product, they often quickly move their eyes to the text in the ad (Rayner et al., 2001). Second, viewers spend more time on implicit ads in which the pictures and text are not directly related to the product than they spend on explicit ads (Radach et al., 2003). Third, although brand names tend to take up little space in an ad, they receive more eye fixations per unit of surface than text or pictures (Wedel & Pieters, 2000). Fourth, viewers tend to spend more time looking at the text portion than at the picture portion of the ad, especially when the proportion of space each takes up is taken into account (Rayner et al., 2001; Wedel & Pieters, 2000). Fifth, viewers typically do not alternate fixations between the text and the picture part of the ad (Rayner et al., 2001, 2008). That is, given that the eyes are in either the text or picture part of the ad, the probability that the next fixation is also in that part of the ad is fairly high (about .75; Rayner et al., 2008). Rayner et al. (2001) found that viewers tended to read the headline or large print, then the smaller print, and then they looked at the picture (although some viewers did an initial cursory scan of the picture). However, Radach et al. (2003) found that their viewers looked back and forth between different elements (often scanning back and forth between the headline, the text, and the picture). Radach et al.

(2003) argued that the differences lie in the fact that the tasks they used were more demanding than those used by Rayner et al. (2001). This brings us to the sixth important point: it is very clear that the goal of the viewer very much influences the pattern of eye movements and how much time viewers spend on different parts of the ad (Pieters & Wedel, 2004; Rayner et al., 2008).

6 Searching through Scenes

As has been described in the previous sections, the online representation of a scene is a critical component of the scene processing, but the task that one is given when looking at a scene is as important to how the scene is processed as the scene's contents itself. Buswell (1935) and Yarbus (1967) both discuss the importance of task in the eye movements that are made when viewing a scene and found that fixations were distributed differently when the task changes (e.g., freely viewing the scene versus searching for people in the scene; see also Castelhano et al., 2009; Torralba et al., 2006). Searching for a specific object in a scene is one of the most common tasks performed both in real life and in the laboratory. Search generally, and search in scenes specifically, involves a combination of what one is looking for (the target) and the environment in which one is looking. Both of these components affect the search individually, and they interact in complex searches like those that occur in real-world scenes. In this section, we will discuss the issues that are involved in searches that occur in scenes, what is generally known about how scene proprieties and target information influence search behavior, the critical interactions of knowledge and stimulus information in search in a scene, and the attempts to apply what has been learned to real-world searches that can have life-and-death outcomes.

The action of a search divides the objects and the areas of the scene into those that are relevant and irrelevant. For the searcher, the division of areas and objects into relevant and irrelevant allows for an efficient search and finding of the desired target. For example, if one is looking for a red book, things that are not red, as well as the ceiling area, can be effectively ignored. On the other hand, objects that are red or book-shaped and surfaces where books normally appear are things and areas that are relevant and likely locations for the target book. Models of visual search tend to use information about the object, the scene, and/or previous knowledge to "guide" the eyes to areas of greater likelihood of a target being located based on target properties. For example, Torralba et al. (2006) described a computational model of search that emphasized scene-contextual information as a driving force. The scene context allowed for top-down knowledge of where targets might be, in addition to bottom-up visual information, to guide attention and the eyes to the target in a scene.

Many studies have shown that the search environment that encompasses the target is critical to the search process. When considering the scenes in which search may occur, many different types of information (horizontal and vertical layout, gist, meaningfulness, saliency, previous experience, etc.) are available that can be exploited.

Objects are distributed across the scene in spatially licensed manner, such that the placement of objects in a scene is not random. For example, objects tend to appear in scenes in areas that are physically licensed and are tied to the object function (Castelhano & Witherspoon, 2016; Greene et al., 2016). Castelhano & Witherspoon (2016) found a strong link between the target object's spatial location and its function within the scene context (see Figure 15). They found that when the functions of novel objects were learned, participants were able to locate them much more quickly than when only the visual features of the target object were known. In a follow-up experiment, they found that when the function was learned, visual search was greatly hampered if the placement of the target object was in a location inconsistent with its stated function than when it was consistent. Both experiments suggest that not only are objects not randomly distributed, but their placement is also tied to how we use them. The distribution of objects within the scene, therefore, may be organized according to the function that they perform in relation to the tasks normally associated with the scene.

Guiding search to the relevant locations is not perfect – the red book mentioned earlier could be taped to the ceiling by a mischievous housemate as a prank – but for the vast majority of searches, the division of relevant and irrelevant regions works well. For researchers, search provides a way to test how attention is deployed through the scene. Researchers may have hypotheses about what should or should not draw attention; these ideas can be put to the test by having searchers try to find what the researchers identify as the target of the search while their eye movements are tracked. Essentially, researchers allow the searchers to indicate what they deem relevant or irrelevant to the search by where and to what the searchers' attention is allocated (see also Williams, 2020).

As mentioned earlier, the Surface Guidance Framework model posits that attention is directed to surfaces in the scene that are most associated with the target. To operationalize target-relevant scene regions, scenes are divided into three horizontal surfaces: (1) upper (e.g., ceiling, upper walls), (2) middle (e.g., countertops, tabletops, desktops, stovetops), and (3) lower (e.g., floor, lower walls). Target-relevant regions are then identified in association with the target

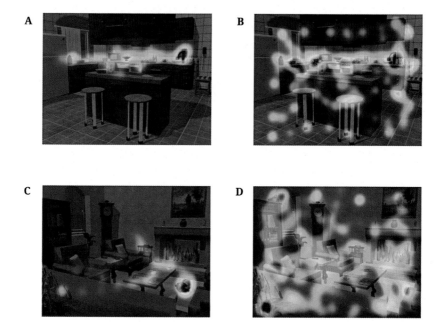

Figure 15 From the Castelhano and Witherspoon (2016) study, the heatmaps in the top row represent the areas of each scene that were fixated on when the object function was studied (A) versus the visual features (B). The bottom row represents the areas of the scene that were fixated on when the target was in a function-consistent location (C) and in a function-inconsistent location (D). See text for details.

object: (1) upper (e.g., painting, hook), (2) middle (e.g., toaster, alarm clock), and (3) lower (e.g., garbage bin, shoes). Using this method of defining each scene and target object combination allows for researchers to divide the scene into target-relevant and target-irrelevant scene regions. This, in turn, allows for the examination of processing differences between relevant and irrelevant scene regions based on spatial expectations of the target object.

Eye-movement measurements are particularly effective at identifying where and for how long particular objects are processed (as described earlier). By identifying the parameters that influence saccades and fixation, researchers can learn more about how different regions of a scene and information therein are prioritized. For example, as mentioned earlier, Pereira and Castelhano (2019) had participants search for a target object where a distractor object would suddenly appear in half of the trials. They found that distractors were much more likely to capture attention when they appeared in target-relevant than target-irrelevant regions. Thus, how attention is deployed is closely tied to the scene structures and their associations with objects.

In another study, Fuggetta, Campana, and Casco (2007) found that implicit knowledge of the structure of a search can facilitate or impair search performance. Object placement is constrained by the properties of the scene and by the laws of physics (normally; Biederman et al., 1973). Objects can be expected to be in reasonable locations for that specific object (e.g., Boettcher et al., 2018; Draschkow & Võ, 2017; Pereira & Castelhano, 2019; Võ et al., 2019). In addition, Neider and Zelinsky (2006b) found that participants' eyes were more likely to fixate on easy-to-segment distractors rather than undefined areas that share target similarity. These results indicate the importance of the ability to identify objects in the environment even when they are detrimental to the task performed. In other words, searchers exploit knowledge about an object and scene to aid in a search.

To further explore the relative importance of the various types of scene information, Koehler and Eckstein (2017) presented manipulated scenes that contained various combinations of cues (background, multiple object configurations, local object co-occurrences). They found that local co-occurrence and object configurations improved search performance in comparison to the background information (see also Pereira and Castelhano, 2014). These results argue for the importance of configuration of objects in a scene. Eckstein (2017) presented an eye-movement model that takes advantage of these probabilistic relationships to predict where the eyes will move in a scene. In general, searchers use information about the environment to help gauge where targets might be located.

Of interest to researchers is also the interaction of the scene context and target. Neider and Zelinsky (2006a) investigated the interaction of target identity and scene composition by having participants search for objects (jeeps or blimps) that were associated with one area or another in a scene (the ground or the air, respectively) while their eye movements were tracked. They found that participants' initial eye movements were toward the area that was expected based on the target given for the search. The initial saccade to the area associated with the target indicates that participants were using their knowledge of the target's properties to guide their eyes to relevant locations of a scene. Castelhano and Heaven (2010) and Malcolm and Henderson (2009) also found that target information and scene information can both contribute independently to finding a target object in the scene. Finally, Spotorno et al. (2013) found that the diagnosticity of an object in a scene and its visual saliency interacted in a change-detection task, supporting the idea that the two systems are not independent of one another.

In order to study the interaction of scene information and target information, one technique that researchers have taken advantage of is the flash preview paradigm (Castelhano & Henderson, 2007). This paradigm involves previewing a scene and then searching that scene for a specified target after a brief presentation of the scene (see Figure 16). Two critical aspects are (1) the target object is specified *after* the scene preview, and (2) the target object is absent from the previewed scene. Frequently, the participant executes a search within a moving window to avoid the influence of peripheral information to the search. Eye tracking during this second presentation of the scene allows the researcher to determine how the scene preview in the absence of target information affects the eye movements in finding the target. Castelhano and Henderson (2007) found that the preview of the scene affected the efficiency of the eye movements to the search target. In other words, participants were using the knowledge of the scene from the preview to aid them in finding the target. When a scene was previewed that did not match the search scene, search eye movements were less efficient. Võ and Henderson (2011) found that even brief glimpses of the correct scene provide enough information to guide the eyes to a target, especially when there is time to integrate that information.

Castelhano and Heaven (2011) used the flash preview paradigm for participants searching in real-world scenes to investigate the interaction of scene semantics and object location in finding the target object. They had participants search for target objects in scenes where they were semantically consistent and

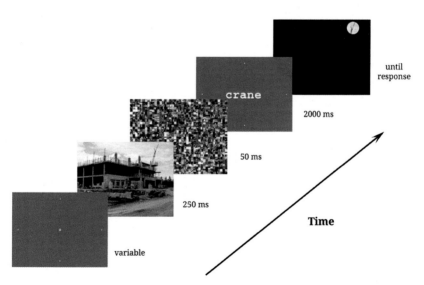

Figure 16 The trial sequence includes a preview of the search scene, the target name, and the search scene, which was viewed through a gaze-contingent window (2° diameter). Taken with permission from Castelhano and Henderson (2007). See text for more details.

scenes where they were semantically inconsistent. In addition, they located the target objects in spatial locations where the target would normally be found or locations where the target would not normally be found. The results indicated that even when objects were in inconsistent scenes, they were still looked for in consistent locations. In other words, similar to Neider and Zelinsky (2006a), information about the target's identity interacted with the scene information to guide the eyes to a reasonable location even when the object is semantically inconsistent with a scene. Spotorno et al. (2014) further investigated how the target template and expected location of the target affected initial saccade in a search. They found more precise target templates (in this case a picture of the actual target) and placing the target in a likely location affected the initial saccade on the scene.

Following a search, what is retained of the memory of the things one is looking for and the environment one is looking at? Tatler and Tatler (2013) found that when performing a task, objects that were relevant to the task were remembered better than expected. In fact, Tatler and Tatler argued that the information extracted/encoded from relevant objects was more efficient than would be expected from fixations alone. Draschkow et al. (2014) examined visual memory for objects in scenes and found that objects that were search targets were remembered better than the same objects when they were just memorized (see also Josephs et al., 2016). However, the memory advantage was limited to when there was a scene background. Critically, these previous studies used a visual recall task (drawing or writing down the names of the objects in the scene). This is in contrast to a recognition task that Williams (2010) used, in which he found that even without the scene background, search targets were remembered better than the same objects when they were memorized. The fact that the scene may have provided additional retrieval cues when no other visual information was present could explain the apparently conflicting findings.

Application in the Real World: Radiology

One of the most notable areas of application of visual search research is in radiology. Radiologists look at x-ray images with the goal of finding an abnormality. To do so, the radiologist must distinguish benign and malignant tumors (Drew et al., 2013; Gandomkar & Mello-Thoms, 2019; Krupinski, 1996; Kundel & Nodine, 1975; Kundel & Wright, 1969; Wolfe et al., 2016, 2017). There are a number of ways in which the search for tumors in radiology parallels the processing found in classic visual search literature. However, of note is the number of additional challenges radiologists must face when searching for a significant abnormality and deciding on a diagnosis.

First, the frequency with which tumors appear is very low and research has shown that across a number of searches, the prevalence of the target across a number of contexts has an effect on the search strategies (Hout et al., 2015; Mitroff et al., 2014; Reed et al., 2011; Wolfe et al., 2005, 2007). There is a tendency to search for less time and for the response to say that no target is present to be more likely (e.g., a change in criteria; Wolfe et al., 2007). The prevalence is thought to change how radiologists search for abnormalities by making it more likely that they will decide on a negative diagnosis (Reed et al., 2011; Wolfe et al., 2007).

In addition, compared to search strategies in a real-world environment (Castelhano & Krzyś, 2020), the spatial placement of tumors is not set and can also occur in areas that are not expected for radiologists (Drew et al., 2013; Hebert et al., 2020; Kundel & Wright, 1969; Williams & Drew, 2019). The narrowing down of a search to certain regions has to be balanced with a need to move to a more thorough and systematic exploration of the stimuli. With new technologies that allow for a 3D representation of the tissue, new strategies can be explored in how radiologists scan and keep track of the spatial regions. Scrolling through depth is thought to allow radiologists to discriminate between tumors and healthy tissue because of the different 3D shapes of these objects (Seltzer et al., 1995). In one study, Drew et al. (2013) examined how viewing volumetric images affected search strategies. In this case, the volumetric images were created by stacking sliced views of the tissue so that radiologists can move through the views in a way that resembles moving through a 3D volume. Interestingly, when examining different strategies for searching across this volumetric space, Drew et al. found two distinct patterns that radiologists tend to adopt: scanners and drillers. Scanners tend to search through a view before moving to a new view at a different depth. On the other hand, drillers hold their eyes in a specific x–y position and quickly scroll through the views across depth. They found no difference in the detection rates for each strategy, although they do note that scanning in 3D volumes generally took longer. Drew et al. attribute part of the increased length of time examining each case to increased difficulty maintaining a representation of what areas have been searched in volumetric space compared to in simple 2D radiographs. Thus, the availability of depth can increase the effectiveness of the examination, but not without some costs.

Another issue in searching for abnormalities is that the target is difficult to define as the radiologist does not know ahead of time what the target looks like. Therefore, many of the processing assumptions about how attention is directed are not as easily applied in this situation because the notion of a target template (the features or characteristics of the target) is much less clear. However, researchers have found that with increased expertise, the distinction between the target and potential targets is easier to ascertain. In recent years, newer technologies have been introduced to incorporate machine learning into identifying abnormalities, as a way of implementing the knowledge gained by experts over years into the software. Computer-Assisted Detection (CAD) automates the identification of potential problem areas for further scrutiny (Cain et al., 2013; Cunningham et al., 2017; Drew et al., 2012; Gandomkar & Mello-Thoms, 2019). CAD systems were originally implemented as a way of easing processing difficulty by highlighting each potential target and thus reducing the amount of time spent on each case. However, more recent studies have pointed to certain problems that arise from the use of CAD systems (Berbaum et al., 2007; Cunningham et al., 2017; Drew et al., 2012; Helbren et al., 2015; Jorritsma et al., 2015; Roos et al., 2010). For instance, in a number of studies, researchers found that the searches are biased toward these highlighted areas of potential targets (Drew et al., 2012; Roos et al., 2010). These studies found that the CAD led to certain biases in responses, such that only areas highlighted for further scrutiny were inspected closely, leading to more misses of abnormalities that were not highlighted by the CAD system. More recent developments have focused on ameliorating the tendency for some to overly rely on the CAD system when making a diagnosis, like soft highlighting of the suspect areas (Kneusel & Mozer, 2017) or delayed display of the CAD highlights (Fazal et al., 2018; Kim et al., 2014). Thus, as the technology advances and becomes more ubiquitous, research shows that the technological advances and the knowledge of experts are not straightforwardly combined.

In addition to these problems, the effectiveness of a search is reduced when more than one abnormality is present in any one case. For instance, Cain, Adamo, and Mitroff (2013) used eye tracking to examine a problem known in radiological search as "satisfaction of search." When searching for possibly multiple targets, satisfaction of search occurs once one target is found; search for other possible targets is then curtailed or impaired. In radiology, satisfaction of search occurs when radiologists find one abnormality, but fail to see a second. Cain et al. found several reasons that could lead to missing targets when multiple targets are present by examining the eye-movement record. Some participants failed to ever fixate on the second target, and other times, the second target was fixated on, but not detected. In other instances, once the primary target was found, the search was terminated (a satisfaction of the search error). Each type of error points to a different cognitive cause of a miss, which indicates multiple processes are involved in producing errors. Visual search as it occurs in applied settings provides an interesting forum to further our understanding of the processes and limitations of human performance across different settings.

7 Spatial Representations and Navigation

One striking difference between scenes and other more simplified stimuli is in the perception of the size and shape of the space of the environment (Castelhano & Krzyś, 2020; Henderson & Hollingworth, 1999; Wolfe, 2020). This can be captured by the size of a depicted environment, but could also be captured by a larger area, not completely captured within a single image (Gibson, 1979; Intraub, 2002; Maguire et al., 2016; Oliva, Wolfe & Arsenio, 2004). In this section, we examine both types of processing – those regarding the perception of space immediately perceptible and the navigation through spaces that involve the immediately proximate spaces as well as the processing of space that is currently out of view. We will first examine how space is first perceived and then how researchers understand the navigation of a larger environment. We first turn to how researchers have examined the navigation of one point to another.

7.1 Spatial Representations

The role of spatial information in memory has been researched extensively for decades, but it remains poorly understood. Here, we will examine (1) how spatial information is stored, (2) how it affects the retrieval of individual objects from memory, and (3) how spatial information of scenes is represented across viewpoints.

Past studies have demonstrated that spatial information can be used as an effective cue for retrieval. For instance, early research demonstrated that associating various types of information with a specific location improved recall (Lea, 1975; Roediger, 1980; Schulman, 1973). In addition, many theories of memory have incorporated space as a unique identifier of different representations (e.g., object file theory: Kahneman et al., 1992; Treisman & Kahneman, 1984). More pertinently, researchers have examined memory for objects within a scene and have shown that location information is both incidentally encoded (Castelhano & Henderson, 2005; Tatler & Land, 2011; Zelinsky & Loschky, 2005) and used as a retrieval cue (Hollingworth, 2005, 2006; Hollingworth & Rasmussen, 2010; Mandler & Ritchey, 1977). For instance, Hollingworth (2006) tested memory for objects viewed within scene images and found better memory performance when the test object was shown in the original position compared to a different position. Likewise, he also found that breaking spatial relations in the scene (scrambled scenes) disrupted the same-location benefit, but the benefit was preserved if the spatial relations were changed but not broken, as with a translation through space. This maintenance of scene context through translation and viewpoint changes suggests a robust and flexible representation of the scene context. Thus, we next turn to the memory of the overall scene across changes in viewpoint.

In the past, how information from multiple viewpoints of a scene is represented in memory was a matter of great debate. As mentioned earlier, Gibson (1979) proposed that navigating through an environment led to a changing vista, with a continual update to overall representation. The nature of place representations is thus contrasted with the representation of the immediate vista and the fluid interchange between these types of representations. An important notion of Gibson's theory was that as one traverses through an environment, there are both the visible and hidden surfaces, each of which need to be represented in order to understand and navigate an environment successfully. The notions of hidden and visible surfaces have been investigated with regards to viewpoint changes of individual objects (e.g., Biederman & Gerhardstein, 1993). Past research on scene processing has largely mirrored research on object recognition, and examining the theoretical approaches to object representations may shed some light on theoretical approaches to scene representations.

Traditionally, theoretical approaches to object recognition across viewpoints fall into two main camps: viewpoint dependent and viewpoint invariant. Researchers who posited a *viewpoint-dependent approach* argued that object representations are largely image-based, where recognition of a new view of an object is based on previous experience (Bülthoff & Bülthoff, 2003; Edelman, 1999; Marr & Poggio, 1979; Tarr & Pinker, 1989; Ullman, 1989). Alternatively, other researchers who supported a *viewpoint-invariant approach* have proposed that the visual system creates a viewpoint-invariant representation of objects. Several past studies have also examined which of the two camps better explained spatial translations and viewpoint changes in scene representations in memory (Castelhano & Pollatsek, 2010; Castelhano, Pollatsek, & Rayner, 2009; Epstein et al., 2007; Waller, Friedman, Hodgson, & Greenauer, 2009).

In one study, Castelhano et al. (2009) had participants study two images prior to an immediate memory test in which they were asked to discriminate between old and new views of the same scene. The two study images were always from two different viewpoints, 40° apart. For the memory test, the distractor images were either an interpolated viewpoint that was 20° from each of the study images or an extrapolated viewpoint that differed by 20° from one of the study images and by 60° from the other (see Figure 17). Participants were less accurate at rejecting interpolated test images than the extrapolated ones, even accounting for view similarity. Conversely, Waller, Friedman, and colleagues (Friedman & Waller, 2008; Waller et al., 2009) found that after extensive training on scene images from multiple viewpoints, an untrained novel view that was taken between the trained views was more easily identified as the same scene than were the trained viewpoints. Taken together, these studies suggest that, under certain circumstances, extrapolation of scene information can be

Study Image 1   Study Image 2   Test

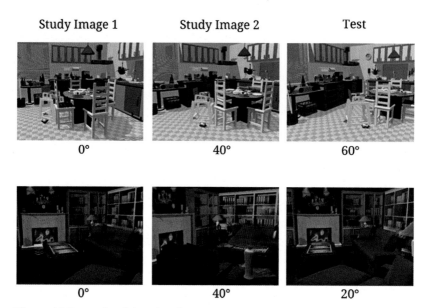

0°   40°   60°

0°   40°   20°

Figure 17 Example of the stimuli used in Castelhano et al. (2009), depicting the environment across different viewpoints. See text for details.

observed. However, it is not clear from these studies what role spatial information in the scenes (especially depth information) played in the generalization and extrapolation of scene layout (as discussed earlier).

Researchers have also examined how different viewpoints are integrated into the spatial representation as you move through the space (Christou & Bülthoff, 1999; Epstein et al., 2007; Waller et al., 2009). In one study, Christou and Bülthoff (1999) used a navigation task in a virtual-reality setting, in which participants explored an attic (consisting of multiple rooms) from certain viewpoints. They found that when participants were asked to recognize still images taken from this environment, scene recognition was highly viewpoint dependent. Nonetheless, recent developments in object recognition have found that depending on the experimental conditions and which parts of the brain examined, one can obtain data supporting both view-invariant and view-based representations (Gauthier & Tarr, 2016). Thus, the relationship between the performance and the type of representation is not the right question. Rather, it is more pertinent to ask which type of information is used when.

7.2 Spatial Processing across Depth and Attentional Processes

In recent years, interest has grown in how information processing across depth impacts attention and memory of scene representations (Bonner & Epstein,

2017, 2018; Fernandes & Castelhano, 2019, 2021; Josephs & Konkle, 2019; Man et al., 2019). Traditionally, studies of depth perception have examined observers' estimates of distance (Cutting & Vishton, 1995; Nagata, 1991) and how information at different distances is processed: from peripersonal to vista space (Costantini et al., 2011; Cutting & Vishton, 1995; Previc, 1998). Researchers have found that there are functionally different types of information available across different categories of depth. Peripersonal space (or personal space) is typically defined as the zone immediately surrounding the observer, generally within arm's reach and slightly beyond (Cutting & Vishton, 1995). This space is thought to be more accurately represented, reflected in higher sensitivity to details and providing a richer source of space information from the local environment.

The immediate impact of objects and agents in the peripersonal area is also thought to lead to increased sensitivity of space, distance, and visual information more generally. For instance, Costantini et al. (2011) examined whether objects would evoke action-related information depending on their apparent distance from the participant. Participants responded as to whether the object presented corresponded to a subsequently presented verb. They found that verbs describing functions of the object were responded to faster when they were within peripersonal space than outside it.

Recent studies on scene processing have also shown qualitatively different processing of spaces closer to the observer (Bonner & Epstein, 2017, 2018; Fernandes & Castelhano, 2021; Josephs & Konkle, 2019; Man et al., 2019). Most recently, Castelhano and Fernandes (2021) found a foreground bias when examining rapid scene perception for images that had mismatched scene categories in the foreground and background (i.e., chimera scenes). That is, foreground information (from the center of the total scene depth to the position of the observer within the scene) had a greater influence on initial scene perception than background information.

Given the qualitative differences in processing across depth, it stands to reason that information closer in depth may have different utility than information farther away, and thus may differently impact eye-movement guidance during visual search in a scene. Indeed, in a recent study, Man, Kryzś, and Castelhano (2019) found a similar foreground bias when examining visual search in these chimera scenes. Targets were placed either closer to the observer (in the foreground of the scene) or farther away (in the background of the scene) and were semantically consistent with only the region in which they were placed. The results showed that even though targets were controlled for size, foreground targets were found more quickly and with fewer fixations than background targets. Thus, it seems reasonable to suggest that the foreground bias is driven by the enhanced processing of visual information physically closer to the observer. Interestingly, this is related to the sequential processing of scene representations as you move through an environment that was mentioned earlier. In this case, the data suggests that the information initially flows from the foreground to the background.

The allocation of attention to a specific point in depth has been shown across numerous tasks (Burgess, Spiers, & Paleologou, 2004; Costantini et al., 2011; Downing & Pinker, 1985; Park & Park, 2018; Previc, 1998; Song, Bennett, Sekuler, & Sun, 2017). For example, using different cueing paradigms, many early studies found an increase in reaction time when invalid cues indicated a different depth than the target (Downing & Pinker, 1985; Gawryszewski et al., 1987). Other studies demonstrated that a unique positioning of a target in a depth plane improved search efficiency (de la Rosa et al., 2008; Finlayson & Grove, 2015; Marrara & Moore, 2000). Researchers also demonstrated that depth information could be used to improve precision of attention allocation. Finlayson and Grove (2015) demonstrated that the efficiency of search is the highest for targets located in the nearest plane, and efficiency declines as the target depth increases. Collectively, these studies established not only that attention can be allocated to a specific location along the z-axis, but also that distractor or irrelevant information is most disruptive when present at the same or near the depth of the target.

Across numerous studies using different stimuli and tasks, researchers have also shown that the processing of information presented closer to an observer is qualitatively different. How depth affects allocation of attention has been examined more extensively within the context of driving. Andersen, Ni, Bian, and Kang (2011) used a standard dot probe paradigm to examine attention. They asked participants to follow a lead vehicle while also monitoring and responding to light changes that were presented at different depths above the roadway. They found that the reaction time to these changes depended both on the horizontal position of the light and the distance from the participant. This is consistent with other studies that have used various type of probes to examine allocation of attention while driving (Gaspar et al., 2016; Rogé et al., 2004).

There is also recent evidence in scene-processing research that the area closer to the observer and within which actions can potentially occur is processed qualitatively differently. Josephs and Konkle (2019) examined the spaces that encompass workspaces within reachable distances, including images depicting a kitchen countertop, a desktop, or a dining table. The surfaces were sized and the objects arranged such that the whole space was actionable or reachable. They found that these spaces were processed in distinct brain regions that differ from both individual objects and larger scene spaces. These findings reinforce the notion that scene information across depths is differently prioritized. Taken together, there is a consistent pattern of prioritization of information closer to an observer – e.g., the foreground bias (Fernandes & Castelhano, 2021) – and it seems reasonable that the depth at which the information occurs would play a role when searching in a real environment. The role of information present in closer spatial proximity introduces an interesting framework from which to consider the nexus of scene processing, navigation, and action. We turn to navigating across an environment next.

7.3 Navigation

Research on navigation has largely focused on understanding how representations allow us to navigate from one point to another (Burgess et al., 2002; Chrastil, 2013; Darken & Peterson, 2014; Maguire et al., 1999). When navigating through an environment, the representation of the scene and space must be updated as one progresses through it (Epstein et al., 1999; Gibson, 1979; Hassabis & Maguire, 2007; He et al., 2013; Maguire, Nannery, & Spiers, 2006). This progression through the environment is also known as wayfinding. In order for wayfinding to be successful, the immediate environment and the knowledge of the larger environment must be integrated continuously.

As you navigate through a space that is larger than the immediately perceptible view, the representation of space is ever evolving. Early on, Gibson (1979) proposed that moving through an environment involves changing vistas: with movement, a new vista opens in front as a former vista closes behind you. Inherent in this notion of evolving representations through space and time is the notion of anticipatory spatial representations (Hubbard, 2005; Intraub, 2010; Spiers & Maguire, 2007; Wirth et al., 2017). Anticipatory spatial representations have an implied continuity of the scene extending beyond the boundaries of the current view of the environment. Intraub (2010) proposed that an anticipatory spatial representation is fundamental to relating individual views of the environment with a map of the larger environment: they ease the processing of new vistas, lead to the integration of successive views, and help to draw attention to unexpected features that occur in an upcoming view.

In addition to the active navigation of a large environmental space, researchers have found that the initial representations of the scene shed light on the affordances of that space (Bonner & Epstein, 2017, 2018; Gibson, 1950, 1979). Gibson (1979) first proposed affordances of scene spaces, which he defined as perceptual properties that indicate potential for action. For instance, as with objects, if a surface is free of obstacles and if the surface texture and structure support walking (a dirt path vs. a river), we instantaneously perceive that the environment affords us a navigational path. Recently, Bonner and Epstein (2017) found that activity in the occipital place area (OPA) is linked to encoding of navigational affordances in a local environment. Interestingly, the patterns of activation allowed for training of a linear decoder to predict navigational affordances of previously unseen scenes, despite the fact that their task was not related to navigation. This suggests that encoding of spatial properties and scene structure relevant to navigation is automatically encoded.

Studies examining scene representations in the brain have also examined representations centered on the anticipatory nature of the 3D structure of scenes (Epstein, Higgins, Jablonski, & Feiler, 2007; Ferrara & Park, 2016; Park, Intraub, Yi, Widders, & Chun, 2007). For instance, in one study, Park et al. (2007) had participants view a close-up image followed by a wide-angle picture and found evidence for spatial extrapolation. The results showed a scene-selective attenuation in certain scene-processing regions such as the parahippo-campal place area (PPA) and retrosplenial cortex (RSC), but no such pattern of extrapolation in the lateral occipital complex (LOC). These findings demonstrated that in areas previously found to correspond to scene processing, scene layout representations were extrapolated beyond the current perceptual input.

Further, the extrapolation of space is evident even with objects and their surrounding space. When examining familiar landmarks, Epstein et al. (2007) found that the PPA responds more strongly to landmarks than to other types objects, suggesting the space around the landmark is represented. More recently, researchers found a connection between an object and the space surrounding it (Collegio et al., 2019; Mullally & Maguire, 2011, 2013). Mullally and Maguire (2013) demonstrated that certain objects (referred to as space-defining objects) evoked depictions of the surrounding three-dimensional space (e.g., oak bed) when they were either viewed or imagined in isolation. This was in contrast to background items (e.g., a floor or a wall) and space-ambiguous objects (e.g., laundry basket), which evoked no such associated spatial representation.

Finally, in addition to how successive views are related across time, research studies have examined how different representations of the environment are spatially related. Environments have been shown to exhibit a hierarchical organization, in which smaller local environments are nested within a larger environment (Hirtle & Jonides, 1985; McNamara, 1986; McNamara et al., 1989). Similarly, studies in scene perception have also shown that subregions of a scene image can be functionally dissociated from the larger scene representation (Brockmole et al., 2006; Brooks et al., 2010; Castelhano et al., 2019). For instance, Castelhano et al. (2019) found that a subregion of a scene could be retrieved independently from the larger context when it was spatially and semantically distinct from the larger context. Thus, it seems reasonable to posit that the way in which subregions are stored is flexible. However, even without active exploration of a place, how spatial representations of scenes are stored in memory has been a topic of much debate over the past few decades.

Application in the Real World: Video Games and Processing the Virtual World

The representation of space of both the immediate visible environment as well as its locations within the larger environment is interesting to both basic and applied research. In one such field, researchers are examining how hours of playing video games has an effect on navigation skills, spatial cognitive abilities, and speed of processing (Choi & Lane, 2013; Green & Bavelier, 2007; Mishra et al., 2011; Powers et al., 2013; Sanchez, 2012; Spence & Feng, 2010; Wu et al., 2012). In one study, Choi and Lane (2013) compared training in a first-person shooter (FPS) game with a third-person shooter (TPS) game. After training for 30 hours, they found that the degree of improvement in spatial attention in the periphery depended on the gaming viewpoint. The results showed the FPS game playing enhanced visual attention ability at both 20° and 30° eccentricity, but this was not seen for the TPS after an equal amount of training time. This led the authors to conclude that video game playing does lead to substantive changes in how attention was allocated over time, but it depended on how the video challenged cognitive processes to adapt. This finding is supported by a number of other studies, such as Mishra et al. (2011), who found differences in selecting targets in the periphery more accurately and faster in individuals with extensive video game-playing experience compared to a group that had little to no experience. Interestingly, this effect was attributed to a more effective suppression of competing signals in the periphery, rather than to an enhanced processing of the task-relevant information.

Many researchers are interested in whether video game playing affects all cognitive processes that generalize across domains, or whether there are specific skills that are developed. For instance, some researchers have found that video game playing may lead to differences in processing and understanding of spatial properties of an environment. In a meta-analysis of video game training, Power et al. (2013) examined spatial imagery in both experienced video game players and novices. They found that while spatial processing was improved overall, the effect on attention and speed of processing was greater. Based on these studies, it is easy to conclude that while many cognitive processes are affected, it is to different extents.

When examining habitual players versus nonplayers, there is always a question of whether there is a certain type of self-selection for those that choose to play video games extensively. Recent research has begun to suggestion that habitual video game players may be drawn to games that reinforce their existing cognitive abilities. For instance, Jaeggi, Buschkuehl, Jonides, and Shah (2011) examined increased general intelligence associated with video game playing. In their study, rather than using a commercially available game, researchers developed their own custom-made video game designed to train nonverbal intelligence. When comparing the different aspects of nonverbal intelligence in individuals trained on this game vs. a control group, they failed to find any significant differences or improvements in nonverbal intelligence. Thus, many researchers point to potential pitfalls of how participants and games are chosen in the literature to try to assess any changes to cognitive processes directly caused by video game play. Nonetheless, this has become an increasingly popular area of research as more applications for these skills are found across a number of careers, including piloting airplanes and surgery.

8 Conclusion

We started this Element by remarking on how traditional inquiries into visual cognition often involve simplified stimuli that are not always easily translatable to processing in the real world. Scene perception encompasses a broad set of known influences on processing, as well as changes to the processes themselves. Based on the works we have discussed, we know that semantics plays a strong role in organizing the information, acting as a scaffolding for newly perceived spaces, as a crutch for weak memories at moments of recall, and as a guide when predicting spaces and places of objects within scenes. We also know that spatial information plays an important role in the organization of items within a scene and in establishing a stable and complete percept of the word. What is less certain are assumptions about the amount of visual detail stored in memory at any one time and whether failures arise from a lack of encoding or poor retrieval of the information. With these certainties and uncertainties about scene perception, we are now entering a new chapter in its investigation. With the development of new technologies – e.g., virtual and augmented realities – many questions remain about how information is processed in immersive environments. As new paradigms and techniques in these interactive spaces are developed, new theoretical questions will present themselves. We look forward to the future conceptualization of visual cognitive processing in real-world scenes.

References

Andersen, G. J., Ni, R., Bian, Z., & Kang, J. (2011). Limits of spatial attention in three-dimensional space and dual-task driving performance. *Accident Analysis & Prevention*, *43*(1), 381–390. https://doi.org/10.1016/j .aap.2010.09.007

Anderson, J. (1996). *The reality of illusion: An ecological approach to cognitive film theory.* Carbondale: Southern Illinois University Press.

Antes, J. R. (1974). The time course of picture viewing. *Journal of Experimental Psychology*, *103*(1), 62–70.

Aribarg, A., & Schwartz, E. M. (2020). Native advertising in online news: Trade-offs among clicks, brand recognition, and website trustworthiness. *Journal of Marketing Research*, *57*(1), 20–34. https://doi.org/10.1177 /0022243719879711

Au-Yeung, S. K., Benson, V., Castelhano, M. S., & Rayner, K. (2011). Eye movement sequences during simple versus complex information processing of scenes in autism spectrum disorder. *Autism Research and Treatment*, *2011*, 1–7. https://doi.org/10.1155/2011/657383

Awh, E., Armstrong, K. M., & Moore, T. (2006). Visual and oculomotor selection: Links, causes and implications for spatial attention. *Trends in Cognitive Sciences*, *10*(3), 124–130. www.sciencedirect.com/science/art icle/pii/S1364661306000167

Awh, E., Belopolsky, A. V., & Theeuwes, J. (2012). Top-down versus bottom-up attentional control: A failed theoretical dichotomy. *Trends in Cognitive Sciences*, *16*(8), 437–443. https://doi.org/10.1016/j.tics.2012.06.010

Bacon-Mace, N., Mace, M. J. M., Fabre-Thorpe, M., & Thorpe, S. J. (2005). The time course of visual processing: Backward masking and natural scene categorisation. *Vision Research*, *45*(11), 1459–1469. https://doi.org/10.1016 /j.visres.2005.01.004

Barhorst-Cates, E. M., Rand, K. M., & Creem-Regehr, S. H. (2016). The effects of restricted peripheral field-of-view on spatial learning while navigating. *PLOS One*, *11*(10), e0163785. https://doi.org/10.1371/journal.pone.0163785

Bassett-Gunter, R. L., Latimer-Cheung, A. E., Martin Ginis, K. A., & Castelhano, M. S. (2014). I spy with my little eye: Cognitive processing of framed physical activity messages. *Journal of Health Communication*, *19*(6), 676–691. https://doi.org/10.1080/10810730.2013.837553

Becker, M. W., Pashler, H., & Lubin, J. (2007). Object-intrinsic oddities draw early saccades. *Journal of Experimental Psychology: Human*

Perception and Performance, *33*(1), 20–30. https://doi.org/10.1037/0096-1523.33.1.20

Benson, V., Castelhano, M. S., Au-Yeung, S. K., & Rayner, K. (2012). Eye movements reveal no immediate "WOW" ("which one's weird") effect in autism spectrum disorder. *Quarterly Journal of Experimental Psychology, 65* (6), 1139–1150. https://doi.org/10.1080/17470218.2011.644305

Benson, V., Castelhano, M. S., Howard, P. L., Latif, N., & Rayner, K. (2016). Looking, seeing and believing in autism: Eye movements reveal how subtle cognitive processing differences impact in the social domain. *Autism Research, 9*(8), 879–887. https://doi.org/10.1002/aur.1580

Benway, J. P., & Lane, D. M. (1998). Banner blindness: Web searchers often miss "obvious" links. Itg Newsletter, 1(3), 1–22.

Berbaum, K. S., Caldwell, R. T., Schartz, K. M., Thompson, B. H., & Franken, E. A. (2007). Does computer-aided diagnosis for lung tumors change satisfaction of search in chest radiography? *Academic Radiology, 14*(9), 1069–1076. https://doi.org/10.1016/j.acra.2007.06.001

Biederman, I. (1972). Perceiving real-world scenes. *Science, 177*(4043), 77–80. https://doi.org/10.1126/SCIENCE.177.4043.77

Biederman, I. (1988). Aspects and extensions of a theory of human image understanding. In Z. Pylyshyn (Ed.), *Computational processes in human vision* (pp. 370–428). Norwood, NJ: Ablex.

Biederman, I., & Gerhardstein, P. C. (1993). Recognizing depth-rotated objects: Evidence and conditions for three-dimensional viewpoint invariance. *Journal of Experimental Psychology: Human Perception and Performance, 19*(6), 1162–1182. https://doi.org/10.1037/0096-1523.19.6.1162

Biederman, I., & Ju, G. (1988). Surface versus edge-based determinants of visual recognition. *Cognitive Psychology, 20*(1), 38–64. https://doi.org/10.1016/0010-0285(88)90024-2

Biederman, I., Glass, A. L., & Stacy, E. W. (1973). Searching for objects in real-world scenes. *Journal of Experimental Psychology, 97*(1), 22–27. https://doi.org/10.1037/h0033776

Bindemann, M. (2010). Scene and screen center bias early eye movements in scene viewing. *Vision Research, 50*(23), 2577–2587. https://doi.org/10.1016/J.VISRES.2010.08.016

Boettcher, S. E. P., Draschkow, D., Dienhart, E., & Võ, M. L.-H. (2018). Anchoring visual search in scenes: Assessing the role of anchor objects on eye movements during visual search. *Journal of Vision, 18*(13), 11. https://doi.org/10.1167/18.13.11

Bonner, M. F., & Epstein, R. A. (2017). Coding of navigational affordances in the human visual system. *Proceedings of the National Academy of Sciences of the United States of America, 114*(18), 4793–4798. https://doi.org/10.1073/pnas.1618228114

Bonner, M. F., & Epstein, R. A. (2018). Computational mechanisms underlying cortical responses to the affordance properties of visual scenes. *PLOS Computational Biology, 14*(4), e1006111. https://doi.org/10.1371/journal.pcbi.1006111

Borji, A., Sihite, D. N., & Itti, L. (2013). Quantitative analysis of human-model agreement in visual saliency modeling: A comparative study. *IEEE Transactions on Image Processing, 22*(1), 55–69. https://doi.org/10.1109/TIP.2012.2210727

Brockmole, J. R., & Henderson, J. M. (2005). Prioritization of new objects in real-world scenes: Evidence from eye movements. *Journal of Experimental Psychology, 31*(5), 857–868.

Brockmole, J. R., & Henderson, J. M. (2006). Using real-world scenes as contextual cues for search. *Visual Cognition, 13*(1), 99–108. https://doi.org/10.1080/13506280500165188

Brockmole, J. R., Castelhano, M. S., & Henderson, J. M. (2006). Contextual cueing in naturalistic scenes: Global and local contexts. *Journal of Experimental Psychology: Learning, Memory, and Cognition, 32*(4), 699–706. https://doi.org/10.1037/0278-7393.32.4.699

Brooks, D. I., Rasmussen, I. P., & Hollingworth, A. (2010). The nesting of search contexts within natural scenes: Evidence from contextual cuing. *Journal of Experimental Psychology. Human Perception and Performance, 36*(6), 1406–1418. https://doi.org/10.1037/a0019257

Bruce, N. D. B., Wloka, C., Frosst, N., & Rahman, S. (2015). On computational modeling of visual saliency: Examining what's right, and what's left. *Vision Research, 116*, 95–112. https://doi.org/10.1016/J.VISRES.2015.01.010

Bülthoff, I., & Bülthoff, H. H. (2003). Image-based recognition of biological motion, scenes, and objects. In M. A. Peterson & G. Rhodes (Eds.), *Perception of faces, objects, and scenes: Analytic and holistic processes* (pp. 146–172). Oxford: Oxford University Press.

Burgess, N., Maguire, E. A., & O'Keefe, J. (2002). The human hippocampus and spatial and episodic memory. *Neuron, 35*(4), 625–641. https://doi.org/10.1016/S0896-6273(02)00830-9

Burgess, N., Spiers, H. J., & Paleologou, E. (2004). Orientational manoeuvres in the dark: Dissociating allocentric and egocentric influences on spatial memory. *Cognition, 94*(2), 149–166. https://doi.org/10.1016/j.cognition.2004.01.001

Buswell, G. (1935). *How people look at pictures: A study of the psychology of perception in art.* Chicago, IL: University of Chicago Press.

Cain, M. S., Adamo, S. H., & Mitroff, S. R. (2013). A taxonomy of errors in multiple-target visual search. *Visual Cognition, 21*(7), 899–921. https://doi.org/10.1080/13506285.2013.843627

Cardwell, B. A., Henkel, L. A., Garry, M., Newman, E. J., & Foster, J. L. (2016). Nonprobative photos rapidly lead people to believe claims about their own (and other people's) pasts. *Memory & Cognition, 44*(6), 883–896. https://doi.org/10.3758/s13421-016-0603-1

Casarotti, M., Lisi, M., Umiltà, C., & Zorzi, M. (2012). Paying attention through eye movements: A computational investigation of the premotor theory of spatial attention. *Journal of Cognitive Neuroscience, 24*(7), 1519–1531. https://doi.org/10.1162/jocn_a_00231

Castelhano, M. S., & Heaven, C. (2010). The relative contribution of scene context and target features to visual search in scenes. *Attention, Perception & Psychophysics, 72*(5), 1283–1297. https://doi.org/10.3758/APP.72.5.1283

Castelhano, M. S., & Heaven, C. (2011). Scene context influences without scene gist: Eye movements guided by spatial associations in visual search. *Psychonomic Bulletin & Review, 18*(5), 890–896. https://doi.org/10.3758/s13423-011-0107-8

Castelhano, M. S., & Henderson, J. M. (2003). Flashing scenes and moving windows: An effect of initial scene gist on eye movements. *Journal of Vision, 3*(9), 67a. https://doi.org/10.1167/3.9.67

Castelhano, M. S., & Henderson, J. M. (2005). Incidental visual memory for objects in scenes. *Visual Cognition, 12*(6), 1017–1040. https://doi.org/10.1080/13506280444000634

Castelhano, M. S., & Henderson, J. M. (2007). Initial scene representations facilitate eye movement guidance in visual search. *Journal of Experimental Psychology: Human Perception and Performance, 33*(4), 753–763. https://doi.org/10.1037/0096-1523.33.4.753

Castelhano, M. S., & Henderson, J. M. (2008a). Stable individual differences across images in human saccadic eye movements. *Canadian Journal of Experimental Psychology = Revue Canadienne de Psychologie Expérimentale, 62*(1), 1–14. https://doi.org/10.1037/1196-1961.62.1.1

Castelhano, M. S., & Henderson, J. M. (2008b). The influence of color on the perception of scene gist. *Journal of Experimental Psychology: Human Perception and Performance, 34*(3), 660–675. https://doi.org/10.1037/0096-1523.34.3.660

Castelhano, M. S., & Krzyś, K. (2020). Rethinking space: A review of perception, attention, and memory in scene processing. *Annual Review of Vision Science, 6*(1), 563–586. https://doi.org/10.1146/annurev-vision-121219-081745

Castelhano, M. S., & Pereira, E. J. (2018). The influence of scene context on parafoveal processing of objects. *Quarterly Journal of Experimental Psychology*, *71*(1), 229–240. https://doi.org/10.1080/17470218 .2017.1310263

Castelhano, M. S., & Pollatsek, A. (2010). Extrapolating spatial layout in scene representations. *Memory Cognition*, *38*(8), 1018–1025.

Castelhano, M. S., & Rayner, K. (2008). Eye movements during reading, visual search, and scene perception: An overview. In K. Rayner, D. Shen, X. Bai, and G. Yan (Eds.), *Cognitive and cultural influences on eye movements* (Vol. 2175, pp. 3–33). Tianjin: Tianjin People's Press/Psychology Press.

Castelhano, M. S., & Witherspoon, R. L. (2016). How you use it matters: Object function guides attention during visual search in scenes. *Psychological Science*, *27*(5), 606–621. https://doi.org/10.1177/0956797616629130

Castelhano, M. S., Fernandes, S., & Theriault, J. (2019). Examining the hierarchical nature of scene representations in memory. *Journal of Experimental Psychology: Learning, Memory, and Cognition*, *45*(9), 1619–1633. https:// doi.org/10.1037/xlm0000660

Castelhano, M. S., Mack, M. L., & Henderson, J. M. (2009). Viewing task influences eye movement control during active scene perception. *Journal of Vision*, *9*(3), 6. https://doi.org/10.1167/9.3.6

Castelhano, M. S., Pollatsek, A., & Cave, K. R. (2008). Typicality aids search for an unspecified target, but only in identification and not in attentional guidance. *Psychonomic Bulletin & Review*, *15*(4), 795–801. https://doi.org /10.3758/PBR.15.4.795

Castelhano, M. S., Pollatsek, A., & Rayner, K. (2009). Integration of multiple views of scenes. *Attention Perception Psychophysics*, *71*(3), 490–502. https://doi.org/10.3758/APP

Castelhano, M. S., Wieth, M., & Henderson, J. M. (2007). I see what you see: Eye movements in real-world scenes are affected by perceived direction of gaze. *Attention in Cognitive Systems Theories and Systems from an Interdisciplinary Viewpoint*, *4840*(9), 251–262. https://doi.org/10.1167/3.9.307

Cavanagh, P., Hunt, A. R., Afraz, A., & Rolfs, M. (2010). Visual stability based on remapping of attention pointers. *Trends in Cognitive Sciences*, *14*(4), 147–153. https://doi.org/10.1016/J.TICS.2010.01.007

Choe, K. W., Kardan, O., Kotabe, H. P., Henderson, J. M., & Berman, M. G. (2017). To search or to like: Mapping fixations to differentiate two forms of incidental scene memory. *Journal of Vision*, *17*(12), 8. https://doi.org/10 .1167/17.12.8

Choi, H. S., & Lane, S. A. (2013). Impact of visuospatial characteristics of video games on improvements in cognitive abilities. *Proceedings of the Human Factors and Ergonomics Society, 57*(1), 1735–1739. https://doi.org/10.1177/1541931213571387

Chrastil, E. R. (2013). Neural evidence supports a novel framework for spatial navigation. *Psychonomic Bulletin and Review, 20*(2), 208–227. https://doi.org/10.3758/s13423-012-0351-6

Christou, C. G., & Bülthoff, H. H. (1999). View dependence in scene recognition after active learning. *Memory & Cognition, 27*(6), 996–1007. https://doi.org/10.3758/BF03201230

Chun, M. M., & Jiang, Y. (1998). Contextual cueing: Implicit learning and memory of visual context guides spatial attention. *Cognitive Psychology, 36* (1), 28–71. https://doi.org/10.1006/cogp.1998.0681

Codispoti, M., De Cesarei, A., & Ferrari, V. (2012). The influence of color on emotional perception of natural scenes. *Psychophysiology, 49*(1), 11–16. https://doi.org/10.1111/j.1469-8986.2011.01284.x

Collegio, A. J., Nah, J. C., Scotti, P. S., & Shomstein, S. (2019). Attention scales according to inferred real-world object size. *Nature Human Behaviour, 3*(1), 40–47. https://doi.org/10.1038/s41562-018-0485-2

Costantini, M., Ambrosini, E., Scorolli, C., & Borghi, A. M. (2011). When objects are close to me: Affordances in the peripersonal space. *Psychonomic Bulletin & Review, 18*(2), 302–308. https://doi.org/10.3758/s13423-011-0054-4

Cronin, D. A., Hall, E. H., Goold, J. E., Hayes, T. R., & Henderson, J. M. (2020). Eye movements in real-world scene photographs: General characteristics and effects of viewing task. *Frontiers in Psychology, 10.* https://doi.org/10.3389/fpsyg.2019.02915

Cunningham, C. A., Drew, T., & Wolfe, J. M. (2017). Analog Computer-Aided Detection (CAD) information can be more effective than binary marks. *Attention, Perception, and Psychophysics, 79*(2), 679–690. https://doi.org/10.3758/s13414-016-1250-0

Cutting, J. E., & Vishton, P. M. (1995). Perceiving layout and knowing distances: The integration, relative potency, and contextual use of different information about depth. In W. Epstein & S. J. Rogers (Eds.), *Handbook of perception and cognition* (2nd ed., pp. 69–117). Cambridge, MA: Academic Press. https://doi.org/10.1016/B978-012240530-3/50005-5

Darken, R., & Peterson, B. (2014). Spatial orientation, wayfinding, and representation. In K. S. Hale and K. M. Stanney (Eds.), *Handbook of virtual environments* (pp. 467–491). Boca Raton, FL: CRC Press. https://doi.org/10.1201/b17360-24

De Graef, P., Christiaens, D., & D'Ydewalle, G. (1990). Perceptual effects of scene context on object identification. *Psychological Research*, *52*(4), 317–329. https://doi.org/10.1007/BF00868064

de la Rosa, S., Moraglia, G., & Schneider, B. A. (2008). The magnitude of binocular disparity modulates search time for targets defined by a conjunction of depth and colour. *Canadian Journal of Experimental Psychology/Revue Canadienne de Psychologie Expérimentale*, *62*(3), 150–155. https://doi.org/10.1037/1196-1961.62.3.150

DeAngelus, M., & Pelz, J. B. (2009). Top-down control of eye movements: Yarbus revisited. *Visual Cognition*, *17*(6–7), 790–811. https://doi.org/10.1080/13506280902793843

Delorme, A., Richard, G., & Fabre-Thorpe, M. (2000). Ultra-rapid categorisation of natural scenes does not rely on colour cues: A study in monkeys and humans. *Vision Research*, *40*(16), 2187–2200. https://doi.org/10.1016/S0042-6989(00)00083-3

Deubel, H., & Schneider, W. X. (1996). Saccade target selection and object recognition: Evidence for a common attentional mechanism. *Vision Research*, *36*(12), 1827–1837. https://doi.org/10.1016/0042-6989(95)00294-4

Deubel, H., Schneider, W. X., & Bridgeman, B. (2002). Transsaccadic memory of position and form. *Progress in Brain Research*, *140*, 165–180. https://doi.org/12508589

Dodhia, R. M., & Metcalfe, J. (1999). False memories and source monitoring. *Cognitive Neuropsychology*, *16*(3–5), 489–508. https://doi.org/10.1080/026432999380898

Dorr, M., Martinetz, T., Gegenfurtner, K. R., & Barth, E. (2010). Variability of eye movements when viewing dynamic natural scenes. *Journal of Vision, 10*(10), 28. https://doi.org/10.1167/10.10.28

Downing, C. J., & Pinker, S. (1985). The spatial structure of visual attention. In M. I. Posner & O. S. M. Martin (Eds.), *Attention and performance XI* (pp. 171–187). Mahwah, NJ: Erlbaum.

Draschkow, D., & Võ, M. L.-H. (2017). Scene grammar shapes the way we interact with objects, strengthens memories, and speeds search. *Scientific Reports*, *7*(1), 16471. https://doi.org/10.1038/s41598-017-16739-x

Draschkow, D., Wolfe, J. M., & Võ, M. L.-H. (2014). Seek and you shall remember: Scene semantics interact with visual search to build better memories. Journal of Vision, 14(8), 1–18. https://doi-org.ezproxy.csusm.edu/10.1167/14.8.10

Drew, T., Cunningham, C., & Wolfe, J. M. (2012). When and why might a computer-aided detection (CAD) system interfere with visual search? An eye-tracking study. *Academic Radiology*, *19*(10), 1260–1267. https://doi.org/10.1016/j.acra.2012.05.013

Drew, T., Võ, M. L.-H., Olwal, A., Jacobson, F., Seltzer, S. E., & Wolfe, J. M. (2013). Scanners and drillers: Characterizing expert visual search through volumetric images. *Journal of Vision*, *13*(10), 3. https://doi.org/10.1167/13.10.3

Eckstein, M. P. (2017). Probabilistic computations for attention, eye movements, and search. *Annual Review of Vision Science*, *3*(1), 319–342. https://doi.org/10.1146/annurev-vision-102016-061220

Edelman, S. (1999). Representation and recognition in vision. *Brain*, 124(5), 1055–1056.

Epstein, R. A., & Baker, C. I. (2019). Scene perception in the human brain. *Annual Review of Vision Science*, *5*(1), 373–397. https://doi.org/10.1146/annurev-vision-091718-014809

Epstein, R. A., Graham, K. S., & Downing, P. E. (2003). Viewpoint-specific scene representations in human parahippocampal cortex. *Neuron*, *37*(5), 865–876.

Epstein, R. A., Higgins, J. S., & Thompson-Schill, S. L. (2005). Learning places from views: Variation in scene processing as a function of experience and navigational ability. *Journal of Cognitive Neuroscience*, *17*(1), 73–83. https://doi.org/10.1162/0898929052879987

Epstein, R. A., Harris, A., Stanley, D., & Kanwisher, N. (1999). The parahippocampal place area: Recognition, navigation, or encoding? *Neuron*, *23*(1), 115–125.

Epstein, R. A., Higgins, J. S., Jablonski, K., & Feiler, A. M. (2007). Visual scene processing in familiar and unfamiliar environments. *Journal of Neurophysiology*, *97*(5), 3670–3683. https://doi.org/10.1152/jn.00003.2007

Erdem, E., & Erdem, A. (2013). Visual saliency estimation by nonlinearly integrating features using region covariances. *Journal of Vision*, *13*(4), 11. https://doi.org/10.1167/13.4.11

Fazal, M. I., Patel, M. E., Tye, J., & Gupta, Y. (2018). The past, present and future role of artificial intelligence in imaging. *European Journal of Radiology*, 105, 246–250. https://doi.org/10.1016/j.ejrad.2018.06.020

Fernandes, S., & Castelhano, M. (2019, July 17). The Foreground Bias: Initial Scene Representations across the Depth Plane. https://doi.org/10.31234/osf.io/s32wz

Fernandes, S., & Castelhano, M. S. (2021). The foreground bias: Initial scene representations across the depth plane. *Psychological Science*, 095679762098446. https://doi.org/10.1177/0956797620984464

Ferrara, K., & Park, S. (2016). Neural representation of scene boundaries. *Neuropsychologia, 89*, 180–190. https://doi.org/10.1016/J.NEUROPSYCHOL OGIA.2016.05.012

Finlayson, N. J., & Grove, P. M. (2015). Visual search is influenced by 3D spatial layout. *Attention, Perception, & Psychophysics, 77*(7), 2322–2330. https://doi.org/10.3758/s13414-015-0924-3

Frey, H.-P., König, P., & Einhäuser, W. (2007). The role of first- and second-order stimulus features for human overt attention. *Perception & Psychophysics, 69*(2), 153–161. https://doi.org/10.3758/BF03193738

Friedman, A. (1979). Framing pictures: The role of knowledge in automatized encoding and memory for gist. *Journal of Experimental Psychology: General, 108*(3), 316–355. https://doi.org/10.1037/0096-3445.108.3.316

Friedman, A., & Waller, D. (2008). View combination in scene recognition. *Memory & Cognition, 36*(3), 467–478. https://doi.org/10.3758/MC.36.3.467

Fuggetta, G., Campana, G., & Casco, C. (2007). The principle of good continuation in space and time can guide visual search in absence of priming or contextual cueing. *Visual Cognition, 15*(7), 834–853.

Gandomkar, Z., & Mello-Thoms, C. (2019). Visual search in breast imaging. *British Journal of Radiology, 92*(1102), 20190057. https://doi.org/10.1259/bjr.20190057

Garry, M., & Gerrie, M. P. (2005). When photographs create false memories. *Current Directions in Psychological Science, 14*(6), 321–325. https://doi.org/10.1111/j.0963-7214.2005.00390.x

Garry, M., & Wade, K. A. (2005). Actually, a picture is worth less than 45 words: Narratives produce more false memories than photographs do. *Psychonomic Bulletin and Review, 12*(2), 359–366. https://doi.org/10.3758/BF03196385

Garsoffky, B., Schwan, S., & Hesse, F. W. (2002). Viewpoint dependency in the recognition of dynamic scenes. *Journal of Experimental Psychology: Learning, Memory and Cognition, 28*(6), 1035–1050.

Gaspar, J. G., Ward, N., Neider, M. B., Crowell, J., Carbonari, R., Kaczmarski, H., Ringer, R. V., Johnson, A. P., Kramer, A. F., & Loschky, L. C. (2016). Measuring the useful field of view during simulated driving with gaze-contingent displays. *Human Factors: The Journal of the Human Factors and Ergonomics Society, 58*(4), 630–641. https://doi.org/10.1177/0018720816642092

Gauthier, I., & Tarr, M. J. (2016). Visual object recognition: Do we (finally) know more now than we did? *Annual Review of Vision Science, 2*(1), 377–396. https://doi.org/10.1146/annurev-vision-111815-114621

Gawryszewski, L. de G., Riggio, L., Rizzolatti, G., & Umiltá, C. (1987). Movements of attention in the three spatial dimensions and the meaning of "neutral" cues. *Neuropsychologia, 25*(1), 19–29. https://doi.org/10.1016/0028-3932(87)90040-6

Gegenfurtner, K. R., & Rieger, J. (2000). Sensory and cognitive contributions of color to the recognition of natural scenes. *Current Biology, 10*(13), 805–808. https://doi.org/10.1016/S0960-9822(00)00563-7

Gibson, J. (1950). *The perception of the visual world.* Boston, MA: Houghton Mifflin. Boston

Gibson, J. J. (1979). *The ecological approach to visual perception.* Boston, MA: Houghton Mifflin.

Gilman, D. (1994). Simplicity, cognition and adaptation: Some remarks on Marr's theory of vision. *PSA: Proceedings of the Biennial Meeting of the Philosophy of Science Association, 1994*(1), 454–464. https://doi.org/10.1086/psaprocbienmeetp.1994.1.193050

Goffaux, V., Jacques, C., Mouraux, A., Oliva, A., Schyns, P. G., & et al. (2005). Diagnostic colours contribute to the early stages of scene categorization: Behavioural and neurophysiological evidence. *Visual Cognition, 12*(6), 878–892.

Gordon, R. D., Vollmer, S. D., & Frankl, M. L. (2008). Object continuity and the transsaccadic representation of form. *Perception & Psychophysics, 70*(4), 667–679. https://doi.org/18556928

Gottesman, C. V. (2011). Mental layout extrapolations prime spatial processing of scenes. *Journal of Experimental Psychology: Human Perception and Performance, 37*(2), 382–395. https://doi.org/10.1037/a0021434

Green, C. S., & Bavelier, D. (2007). Action-video-game experience alters the spatial resolution of vision. *Psychological Science, 18*(1), 88–94. https://doi.org/10.1111/j.1467-9280.2007.01853.x

Greene, M. R., & Oliva, A. (2009a). Recognition of natural scenes from global properties: Seeing the forest without representing the trees. *Cognitive Psychology, 58*(2), 137–176. https://doi.org/10.1016/j.cogpsych.2008.06.001

Greene, M. R., & Oliva, A. (2009b). The briefest of glances: The time course of natural scene understanding. *Psychological Science, 20*(4), 464–472. https://doi.org/10.1111/j.1467-9280.2009.02316.x

Greene, M. R., & Oliva, A. (2010). High-level aftereffects to global scene properties. *Journal of Experimental Psychology: Human Perception and Performance, 36*(6), 1430–1442. https://doi.org/10.1037/a0019058

Greene, M. R., & Wolfe, J. M. (2011). Global image properties do not guide visual search. *Journal of Vision, 11*(6), 1–9.

Greene, M. R., Baldassano, C., Esteva, A., Beck, D. M., & Fei-Fei, L. (2016). Visual scenes are categorized by function. *Journal of Experimental Psychology: General, 145*(1), 82–94. https://doi.org/10.1037/xge0000129

Grimes, J. A. (1996). On the failure to detect changes in scenes across saccades. In K. A. Akins (Ed.), *Perception: Vancouver Studies in Cognitive Science* (pp. 89–110). Oxford: Oxford University Press.

Gronau, N., & Shachar, M. (2015). Contextual consistency facilitates long-term memory of perceptual detail in barely seen images. *Journal of Experimental Psychology: Human Perception and Performance, 41*(4), 1095–1111. https://doi.org/10.1037/xhp0000071

Haji-Abolhassani, A., & Clark, J. J. (2014). An inverse Yarbus process: Predicting observers' task from eye movement patterns. *Vision Research, 103*, 127–142. https://doi.org/10.1016/j.visres.2014.08.014

Hassabis, D., & Maguire, E. A. (2007). Deconstructing episodic memory with construction. *Trends in Cognitive Sciences, 11*(7), 299–306.

He, C., Peelen, M. V., Han, Z., Lin, N., Caramazza, A., & Bi, Y. (2013). Selectivity for large nonmanipulable objects in scene-selective visual cortex does not require visual experience. *NeuroImage, 79*, 1–9. https://doi.org/10.1016/j.neuroimage.2013.04.051

Hebert, C. R., Sha, L. Z., Remington, R. W., & Jiang, Y. V. (2020). Redundancy gain in visual search of simulated X-ray images. *Attention, Perception, and Psychophysics, 82*, 1–13. https://doi.org/10.3758/s13414-019-01934-x

Hecht, H., & Kalkofen, H. (2009). Questioning the rules of continuity editing: An empirical study. *Empirical Studies of the Arts, 27*(1), 1–23. https://doi.org/10.2190/em.27.1.aa

Heidenreich, S. M., & Turano, K. A. (2011). Where does one look when viewing artwork in a museum? *Empirical Studies of the Arts, 29*(1), 51–72. https://doi.org/10.2190/EM.29.1.d

Helbren, E., Phillips, P., & Altman, D. (2015). The effect of computer-aided detection markers on visual search and reader performance during concurrent reading of CT colonography. *Springer, 25*(6), 1570–1578. https://doi.org/10.1007/s00330-014-3569-z

Henderson, J. M. (2003). Human gaze control during real-world scene perception. *Trends in Cognitive Sciences, 7*(11), 498–504. https://doi.org/10.1016/j.tics.2003.09.006

Henderson, J. M., & Castelhano, M. S. (2005). Eye movements and visual memory for scenes. In G. Underwood (Ed.), *Cognitive processes in eye guidance* (pp. 213–235). Oxford: Oxford University Press.

Henderson, J. M., & Hayes, T. R. (2017). Meaning-based guidance of attention in scenes as revealed by meaning maps. *Nature Human Behaviour, 1*(10), 743–747. https://doi.org/10.1038/s41562-017-0208-0

Henderson, J. M., Weeks, P. A. J., & Hollingworth, A. (1999). The effects of semantic consistency on eye movements during complex scene viewing. *Journal of Experimental Psychology: Human Perception and Performance, 25*(1), 210–228. https://doi.org/10.1037/0096-1523.25.1.210

Henderson, J. M., Williams, C. C., Castelhano, M. S., & Falk, R. J. (2003). Eye movements and picture processing during recognition. *Perception & Psychophysics*, *65*(5), 725–734. https://doi.org/10.3758/BF03194809

Henderson, J. M., Brockmole, J. R., Castelhano, M. S., & Mack, M. (2007). Visual saliency does not account for eye movements during visual search in real-world scenes. In R. van Gompel, M. Fischer, W. S. Murray, & R. L. Hill (Eds.), *Eye movements: A window on mind and brain* (pp. 537–562). New York: Elsevier. https://doi.org/10.1016/B978-008044980-7/50027-6

Henderson, J. M., Shinkareva, S. V., Wang, J., Luke, S. G., & Olejarczyk, J. (2013). Predicting cognitive state from eye movements. *PLoS ONE*, *8*(5), e64937. https://doi.org/10.1371/journal.pone.0064937

Henkel, L. A., & Milliken, A. (2020). The benefits and costs of editing and reviewing photos of one's experiences on subsequent memory. *Journal of Applied Research in Memory and Cognition*, *9*(4), 480–494. https://doi.org/10.1016/j.jarmac.2020.07.002

Hervet, G., Guérard, K., Tremblay, S., & Chtourou, M. S. (2011). Is banner blindness genuine? Eye tracking internet text advertising. *Applied Cognitive Psychology*, *25*(5), 708–716. https://doi.org/10.1002/acp.1742

Higgins, E., Leinenger, M., & Rayner, K. (2014). Eye movements when viewing advertisements. *Frontiers in Psychology*, *5*(Mar), 210. https://doi.org/10.3389/fpsyg.2014.00210

Hinde, S. J., Smith, T. J., & Gilchrist, I. D. (2017). In search of oculomotor capture during film viewing: Implications for the balance of top-down and bottom-up control in the saccadic system. *Vision Research*, *134*, 7–17.

Hirtle, S. C., & Jonides, J. (1985). Evidence of hierarchies in cognitive maps. *Memory & Cognition*, *13*(3), 208–217. https://doi.org/10.3758/BF03197683

Hoffman, J. E., & Subramaniam, B. (1995). The role of visual attention in saccadic eye movements. *Perception & Psychophysics*, *57*, 787.

Hollingworth, A. (2004). Constructing visual representations of natural scenes: The roles of short- and long-term visual memory. *Journal of Experimental Psychology. Human Perception and Performance*, *30*(3), 519–537. https://doi.org/10.1037/0096-1523.30.3.519

Hollingworth, A. (2005). Memory for object position in natural scenes. *Visual Cognition*, *12*(6), 1003–1016.

Hollingworth, A. (2006). Scene and position specificity in visual memory for objects. *Journal of Experimental Psychology Learning Memory and Cognition*, *32*(1), 58.

Hollingworth, A., & Henderson, J. M. (2000). Semantic informativeness mediates the detection of changes in natural scenes. *Change Blindness and Visual Memory, 2000*(7), 213–235.

Hollingworth, A., & Henderson, J. M. (2002). Accurate Visual memory for previously attended objects in natural scenes. *Journal of Experimental Psychology Human Perception and Performance, 28*(1), 113–136.

Hollingworth, A., & Rasmussen, I. P. (2010). Binding objects to locations: The relationship between object files and visual working memory. *Journal of Experimental Psychology: Human Perception and Performance, 36*(3), 543–564. https://doi.org/10.1037/a0017836

Hollingworth, A., Williams, C. C., & Henderson, J. M. (2001). To see and remember: Visually specific information is retained in memory from previously attended objects in natural scenes. *Psychonomic Bulletin & Review, 8* (4), 761–768. https://doi.org/10.3758/BF03196215

Hout, M. C., & Goldinger, S. D. (2012). Incidental learning speeds visual search by lowering response thresholds, not by improving efficiency: Evidence from eye movements. *Journal of Experimental Psychology: Human Perception and Performance, 38*(1), 90–112. https://doi.org/10.1037/a0023894

Hout, M. C., Walenchok, S. C., Goldinger, S. D., & Wolfe, J. M. (2015). Failures of perception in the low-prevalence effect: Evidence from active and passive visual search. *Journal of Experimental Psychology: Human Perception and Performance, 41*(4), 977–994. https://doi.org/10.1037/xhp0000053

Hristova, E., Georgieva, S., & Grinberg, M. (2011). Top-down influences on eye-movements during painting perception: The effect of task and titles. *Lecture Notes in Computer Science (Including Subseries Lecture Notes in Artificial Intelligence and Lecture Notes in Bioinformatics), 6456 LNCS,* 104–115. https://doi.org/10.1007/978-3-642-18184-9_10

Hubbard, T. L. (2005). Representational momentum and related displacements in spatial memory: A review of the findings. *Psychonomic Bulletin and Review, 12*(5), 822–851. https://doi.org/10.3758/BF03196775

Hutson, J. P., Smith, T. J., Magliano, J. P., & Loschky, L. C. (2017). What is the role of the film viewer? The effects of narrative comprehension and viewing task on gaze control in film. *Cognitive Research: Principles and Implications, 2*(1), 46. https://doi.org/10.1186/s41235-017-0080-5

Hwang, A. D., Wang, H.-C., & Pomplun, M. (2011). Semantic guidance of eye movements in real-world scenes. *Vision Research, 51*(10), 1192–1205. https://doi.org/10.1016/j.visres.2011.03.010

Ildirar, S., & Schwan, S. (2015). First-time viewers' comprehension of films: Bridging shot transitions. *British Journal of Psychology, 106*(1), 133–151. https://doi.org/10.1111/bjop.12069

Intraub, H. (2010). Rethinking scene perception: A multisource model. *Psychology of Learning and Motivation, 52,* 231–264. https://doi.org/10 .1016/S0079-7421(10)52006-1

Intraub, H. (2012). Rethinking visual scene perception. *Wiley Interdisciplinary Reviews: Cognitive Science, 3*(1), 117–127. https://doi.org/10.1002/wcs.149

Intraub, H., & Richardson, M. (1989). Wide-angle memories of close-up scenes. *Journal of Experimental Psychology: Learning, Memory, and Cognition, 15*(2), 179–187. https://doi.org/10.1037//0278-7393.15.2.179

Intraub, H., Gottesman, C. V., & Bills, A. J. (1998). Effects of perceiving and imagining scenes on memory for pictures. *Journal of Experimental Psychology: Learning, Memory, and Cognition, 24*(1), 186–201. https://doi .org/10.1037/0278-7393.24.1.186

Itti, L., & Koch, C. (2000). A saliency-based search mechanism for overt and covert shifts of visual attention. *Vision Research, 40*(10–12), 1489–1506.

Itti, L., Koch, C., & Niebur, E. (1998). A model of saliency-based visual attention for rapid scene analysis. *IEEE Transactions on Pattern Analysis and Machine Intelligence, 20*(11), 1254–1259. https://doi.org/10.1109/34.730558

Jaeggi, S. M., Buschkuehl, M., Jonides, J., & Shah, P. (2011). Short-and long-term benefits of cognitive training. Proceedings of the National Academy of Sciences, 108(25), 10081–10086.

Jorritsma, W., Cnossen, F., & van Ooijen, P. M. A. (2015). Improving the radiologist–CAD interaction: Designing for appropriate trust. *Clinical Radiology, 70*(2), 115–122. https://doi.org/10.1016/j.crad.2014.09.017

Joseph, J. E., & Proffitt, D. R. (1996). Semantic versus perceptual influences of color in object recognition. *Journal of Experimental Psychology: Learning, Memory, and Cognition, 22*(2), 407–429. https://doi.org/10.1037/0278-7393.22.2.407

Josephs, E. L., & Konkle, T. (2019). Perceptual dissociations among views of objects, scenes, and reachable spaces. *Journal of Experimental Psychology: Human Perception and Performance, 45*(6), 715–728. https://doi.org/10 .1037/xhp0000626

Josephs, E., Drew, T., & Wolfe, J. (2016). Shuffling your way out of change blindness. *Psychonomic Bulletin & Review, 23*(1), 193–200. https://doi.org /10.3758/s13423-015-0886-4

Josephs, E. L., Draschkow, D., Wolfe, J. M., & Võ, M. L.-H. (2016). Gist in time: Scene semantics and structure enhance recall of searched objects. *Acta Psychologica, 169,* 100–108. https://doi.org/10.1016/ J.ACTPSY.2016.05.013

Kahneman, D., Treisman, A., & Gibbs, B. J. (1992). The reviewing of object files: Object-specific integration of information. *Cognitive Psychology, 24* (2), 175–219. https://doi.org/10.1016/0010-0285(92)90007-O

Kanan, C., Tong, M. H., Zhang, L., & Cottrell, G. W. (2009). SUN: Top-down saliency using natural statistics. *Visual Cognition*, *17*(6–7), 979–1003. https://doi.org/10.1080/13506280902771138

Kim, Y. W., Mansfield, L. T., & Mansfield, L. T. (2014). Fool me twice: Delayed diagnoses in radiology with emphasis on perpetuated errors. *American Journal of Roentgenology*, *202*(3), 465–470. https://doi.org/10.2214/AJR.13.11493

Kneusel, R. T., & Mozer, M. C. (2017). Improving human-machine cooperative visual search with soft highlighting. *ACM Trans. Appl. Percept*, *15*(3), 1–21. https://doi.org/10.1145/3129669

Koehler, K., & Eckstein, M. M. P. M. (2017). Beyond scene gist: Objects guide search more than scene background. *Journal of Experimental Psychology*, *43* (6), 1177–1193. https://doi.org/10.1037/xhp0000363

Konkle, T., & Brady, T. (2010). Conceptual distinctiveness supports detailed visual long-term memory for real-world objects. *Journal of Experimental Psychology.*

Konkle, T., Brady, T. F., Alvarez, G. A., & Oliva, A. (2010). Scene memory is more detailed than you think: The role of categories in visual long-term memory. *Psychological Science*, *21*(11), 1551–1556. https://doi.org/10 .1177/0956797610385359

Krupinski, E. A. (1996). Visual scanning patterns of radiologists searching mammograms. *Academic Radiology*, *3*(2), 137–144. https://doi.org/10.1016 /S1076-6332(05)80381-2

Kundel, H. L., & Nodine, C. F. (1975). Interpreting chest radiographs without visual search. *Radiology*, *116*(3), 527–532. https://doi.org/10.1148/116.3.527

Kundel, H. L., & Wright, D. J. (1969). The influence of prior knowledge on visual search strategies during the viewing of chest radiographs. *Radiology*, *93*(2), 315–320. https://doi.org/10.1148/93.2.315

Land, M. F., & Hayhoe, M. (2001). In what ways do eye movements contribute to everyday activities? *Vision Research*, *41*(25–26), 3559–3565. https://doi .org/10.1016/S0042-6989(01)00102-X

LaPointe, M. R. P., & Milliken, B. (2016). Semantically incongruent objects attract eye gaze when viewing scenes for change. *Visual Cognition*, *24*(1), 63–77. https://doi.org/10.1080/13506285.2016.1185070

LaPointe, M. R. P., Lupianez, J., & Milliken, B. (2013). Context congruency effects in change detection: Opposing effects on detection and identification. *Visual Cognition*, *21*(1), 99–122. https://doi.org/10.1080/13506285 .2013.787133

Larson, A. M., & Loschky, L. C. (2009). The contributions of central versus peripheral vision to scene gist recognition. *Journal of Vision*, *9*(10), 6. https:// doi.org/10.1167/9.10.6

Latif, N., Gehmacher, A., Castelhano, M. S., & Munhall, K. G. (2014). The art of gaze guidance. *Journal of Experimental Psychology: Human Perception and Performance, 40*(1), 33–39. https://doi.org/10.1037/a0034932

Lea, G. (1975). Chronometric analysis of the method of loci. *Journal of Experimental Psychology: Human Perception and Performance, 1*(2), 95–104. https://doi.org/10.1037/0096-1523.1.2.95

Li, C.-L., Aivar, M. P., Kit, D. M., Tong, M. H., & Hayhoe, M. M. (2016). Memory and visual search in naturalistic 2D and 3D environments. *Journal of Vision, 16*(8), 9. https://doi.org/10.1167/16.8.9

Li, F. F., Iyer, A., Koch, C., & Perona, P. (2007). What do we perceive in a glance of a real-world scene? *Journal of Vision, 7*(1), 10. https://doi.org/10.1167/7.1.10

Lindsay, D. S., Hagen, L., Read, J. D., Wade, K. A., & Garry, M. (2004). True photographs and false memories. *Psychological Science, 15*(3), 149–154. https://doi.org/10.1111/j.0956-7976.2004.01503002.x

Liv, N., & Greenbaum, D. (2020). Deep fakes and memory malleability: False memories in the service of fake news. *AJOB Neuroscience, 11*(2), 96–104. https://doi.org/10.1080/21507740.2020.1740351

Loftus, E. F. (2019). Eyewitness testimony. *Applied Cognitive Psychology, 33*(4), acp.3542. https://doi.org/10.1002/acp.3542

Loftus, G. R., & Mackworth, N. H. (1978). Cognitive determinants of fixation location during picture viewing. *Journal of Experimental Psychology: Human Perception and Performance, 4*(4), 565–572. https://doi.org/10.1037/0096-1523.4.4.565

Loschky, L. C., Larson, A. M., Magliano, J. P., & Smith, T. J. (2015). What would Jaws do? The tyranny of film and the relationship between gaze and higher-level narrative film comprehension. *PLoS ONE, 10*(11), e0142474. https://doi.org/10.1371/journal.pone.0142474

Loschky, L. C., Larson, A. M., Smith, T. J., & Magliano, J. P. (2020). The Scene Perception & Event Comprehension Theory (SPECT) applied to visual narratives. *Topics in Cognitive Science, 12*(1), 311–351. https://doi.org/10.1111/tops.12455

Macé, M. J. M., Delorme, A., Richard, G., & Fabre-Thorpe, M. (2010). Spotting animals in natural scenes: Efficiency of humans and monkeys at very low contrasts. *Animal Cognition, 13*(3), 405–418. https://doi.org/10.1007/s10071-009-0290-4

Mack, S. C., & Eckstein, M. P. (2011). Object co-occurrence serves as a contextual cue to guide and facilitate visual search in a natural viewing environment. *Journal of Vision, 11*(9), 9. https://doi.org/10.1167/11.9.9

Mackworth, N. H., & Morandi, A. J. (1967). The gaze selects informative details within pictures. *Perception & Psychophysics*, *2*(11), 547–552. https://doi.org/10.3758/BF03210264

Magliano, J. P., & Zacks, J. M. (2011). The impact of continuity editing in narrative film on event segmentation. *Cognitive Science*, *35*(8), 1489–1517. https://doi.org/10.1111/j.1551-6709.2011.01202.x

Maguire, E. A., Intraub, H., & Mullally, S. L. (2016). Scenes, spaces, and memory traces. *The Neuroscientist*, *22*(5), 432–439. https://doi.org/10.1177/1073858415600389

Maguire, E. A., Nannery, R., & Spiers, H. J. (2006). Navigation around London by a taxi driver with bilateral hippocampal lesions. *Brain*, *129*(11), 2894–2907. https://doi.org/10.1093/brain/awl286

Maguire, E. A., Burgess, N., O'Keefe, J., & O'Keefe, J. (1999). Human spatial navigation: Cognitive maps, sexual dimorphism, and neural substrates. *Current Opinion in Neurobiology*, *9*(2), 171–177. https://doi.org/10.1016/S0959-4388(99)80023-3

Malcolm, G. L., & Henderson, J. M. (2009). The effects of target template specificity on visual search in real-world scenes: Evidence from eye movements. *Journal of Vision*, *9*(11), 8.1–13. https://doi.org/10.1167/9.11.8

Malcolm, G. L., & Henderson, J. M. (2010). Combining top-down processes to guide eye movements during real-world scene search. *Journal of Vision*, *10*(2), 4.1–11. https://doi.org/10.1167/10.2.4

Man, L. L. Y., Krzys, K., & Castelhano, M. (2019, October 22). The Foreground Bias: Differing impacts across depth on visual search in scenes. https://doi.org/10.31234/osf.io/w6j4a

Mandler, J. M., & Johnson, N. S. (1976). Some of the thousand words a picture is worth. *Journal of Experimental Psychology: Human Learning and Memory*, *2*(5), 529–540. https://doi.org/10.1037/0278-7393.2.5.529

Mandler, J. M., & Ritchey, G. H. (1977). Long-term memory for pictures. *Journal of Experimental Psychology: Human Learning & Memory*, *3*(4), 386. https://doi.org/10.1037/0278-7393.3.4.386

Mapelli, D., & Behrmann, M. (1997). The role of color in object recognition: Evidence from visual agnosia. *Neurocase*, *3*(4), 237–247. https://doi.org/10.1080/13554799708405007

Margarida Barreto, A. (2013). Do users look at banner ads on Facebook? *Journal of Research in Interactive Marketing*, *7*(2), 119–139. https://doi.org/10.1108/JRIM-Mar-2012-0013

Marr, D., & Poggio, B. T. (1979). A computational theory of human stereo vision. *Proceedings of the Royal Society of London. Series B. Biological Sciences*, *204*(1156), 301–328. https://doi.org/10.1098/rspb.1979.0029

Marrara, M. T., & Moore, C. M. (2000). Role of perceptual organization while attending in depth. *Perception & Psychophysics*, *62*(4), 786–799. https://doi .org/10.3758/BF03206923

McConkie, G. W., & Zola, D. (1979). Is visual information integrated across successive fixations in reading? *Perception & Psychophysics*, *25*(3), 221–224. https://doi.org/10.3758/BF03202990

McNamara, T. P. (1986). Mental representations of spatial relations. *Cognitive Psychology*, *18*(1), 87–121. https://doi.org/10.1016/0010-0285(86)90016-2

McNamara, T. P., Hardy, J. K., & Hirtle, S. C. (1989). Subjective hierarchies in spatial memory. *Journal of Experimental Psychology: Learning, Memory, and Cognition*, *15*(2), 211–227. https://doi.org/10.1037/0278-7393.15.2.211

Mills, M., Hollingworth, A., Van der Stigchel, S., Hoffman, L., & Dodd, M. D. (2011). Examining the influence of task set on eye movements and fixations. *Journal of Vision*, *11*(8), 17. https://doi.org/10.1167/11.8.17

Mishra, J., Zinni, M., Bavelier, D., & Hillyard, S. A. (2011). Neural basis of superior performance of action videogame players in an attention-demanding task. *Journal of Neuroscience*, *31*(3), 992–998. https://doi.org/10.1523 /JNEUROSCI.4834-10.2011

Mitroff, S., & Biggs, A. T. (2014). The ultra-rare-item effect: Visual search for exceedingly rare items is highly susceptible to error. *Psychological Science*, *25*(1), 284–289. https://doi.org/10.1177/0956797613504221

Mullally, S. L., & Maguire, E. A. (2011). A new role for the parahippocampal cortex in representing space. *The Journal of Neuroscience: The Official Journal of the Society for Neuroscience*, *31*(20), 7441–7449. https://doi.org /10.1523/JNEUROSCI.0267-11.2011

Mullally, S. L., & Maguire, E. A. (2013). Exploring the role of space-defining objects in constructing and maintaining imagined scenes. *Brain and Cognition*, *82*(1), 100–107. https://doi.org/10.1016/J.BANDC.2013.02.013

Murch, W. (2001). *In the blink of an eye*. Hollywood, CA: Silman-James Press.

Murphy, G., Loftus, E. F., Grady, R. H., Levine, L. J., & Greene, C. M. (2019). False memories for fake news during Ireland's abortion referendum. *Psychological Science*, *30*(10), 1449–1459. https://doi.org/10.1177 /0956797619864887

Nagata, S. (1991). How to reinforce perception of depth in single 2-D pictures. In S. Ellis (Ed.), *Pictorial Communication in Virtual and Real Environments* (1st ed., pp. 527–545). London: Taylor & Francis. https://doi.org/10.1201/ 9781482295177

Nash, R. A. (2018). Changing beliefs about past public events with believable and unbelievable doctored photographs. *Memory, 26*(4), 439–450. https://doi.org/10.1080/09658211.2017.1364393

Neider, M. B., & Zelinsky, G. J. (2006a). Scene context guides eye movements during visual search. *Vision Research, 46*(5), 614–621. https://doi.org/10.1016/j.visres.2005.08.025

Neider, M. B., & Zelinsky, G. J. (2006b). Searching for camouflaged targets: Effects of target-background similarity on visual search. *Vision Research, 46*(14), 2217–2235. https://doi-org.ezproxy.csusm.edu/10.1016/j.visres.2006.01.006

Neisser, U., & Kerr, N. (1973). Spatial and mnemonic properties of visual images. *Cognitive Psychology, 5*(2), 138–150. https://doi.org/10.1016/0010-0285(73)90030-3

Newman, E. J., Jalbert, M. C., Schwarz, N., & Ly, D. P. (2020). Truthiness, the illusory truth effect, and the role of need for cognition. *Consciousness and Cognition, 78*, 102866. https://doi.org/10.1016/j.concog.2019.102866

Nichols, R. M., & Loftus, E. F. (2019). Who is susceptible in three false memory tasks? *Memory, 27*(7), 962–984. https://doi.org/10.1080/09658211.2019.1611862

Nickerson, R. S. (1965). Short-term memory for complex meaningful visual configurations: A demonstration of capacity. *Canadian Journal of Psychology/Revue Canadienne de Psychologie, 19*(2), 155–160. https://doi.org/10.1037/h0082899

Nickerson, R. S. (1968). A note on long-term recognition memory for pictorial material. *Psychonomic Science, 11*(2), 58. https://doi.org/10.3758/BF03330991

Nijboer, T. C. W., Kanai, R., De Haan, E. H. F., Van Der Smagt, M. J., & de Hann, E. H. F. (2008). Recognising the forest, but not the trees: An effect of colour on scene perception and recognition. *Consciousness and Cognition, 17*(3), 741–752. https://doi.org/10.1016/j.concog.2007.07.008.

Nuthmann, A. (2017). Fixation durations in scene viewing: Modeling the effects of local image features, oculomotor parameters, and task. *Psychonomic Bulletin & Review, 24*(2), 370–392. https://doi.org/10.3758/s13423-016-1124-4

Nuthmann, A., & Malcolm, G. L. (2016). Eye guidance during real-world scene search: The role color plays in central and peripheral vision. *Journal of Vision, 16*(2), 3. https://doi.org/10.1167/16.2.3

Oliva, A. (2005). Gist of the scene. In L. Itti, G. Rees, & J. K. Tsotsos (Eds.), *Neurobiology of attention* (pp. 251–256). New York: Academic Press. https://doi.org/10.1016/B978-012375731-9/50045-8

Oliva, A., & Schyns, P. G. (1997). Coarse blobs or fine edges? Evidence that information diagnosticity changes the perception of complex visual stimuli. *Cognitive Psychology, 34*(1), 72–107.

Oliva, A., & Schyns, P. G. (2000). Diagnostic colors mediate scene recognition. *Cognitive Psychology, 41*(2), 176–210. https://doi.org/10.1006/cogp.1999.0728

Oliva, A., & Torralba, A. (2001). Modeling the shape of the scene: A holistic representation of the spatial envelope. *International Journal of Computer Vision, 42*(3), 145–175.

Oliva, A., & Torralba, A. (2007). The role of context in object recognition. *Trends in Cognitive Sciences, 11*(12), 520–527. https://doi.org/10.1016/j.tics.2007.09.009

Oliva, A., Torralba, A., Castelhano, M. S., & Henderson, J. M. (2003). Top-down control of visual attention in object detection. *IEEE International Conference on Image Processing, 1*(9), 253–256. https://doi.org/10.1167/3.9.3

Oliva, A., Wolfe, J. M., & Arsenio, H. C. (2004). Panoramic search: the interaction of memory and vision in search through a familiar scene. Journal of experimental psychology: Human perception and performance, 30(6), 1132–1146.

O'Regan, J. (1992). Solving the "real" mysteries of visual perception: The world as an outside memory. *Canadian Journal of Psychology/Revue Canadienne, 46*(3), 461–488.

O'Regan, J., & Noë, A. (2001). A sensorimotor account of vision and visual consciousness. *Behavioral and Brain Sciences, 24*(5), 939–973.

O'Regan, J., Rensink, R., & Clark, J. (1999). Change-blindness as a result of "mudsplashes." *Nature, 398*, 34.

Pannasch, S., & Velichkovsky, B. M. (2009). Distractor effect and saccade amplitudes: Further evidence on different modes of processing in free exploration of visual images. *Visual Cognition, 17*(6–7), 1109–1131. https://doi.org/10.1080/13506280902764422

Park, J., & Park, S. (2018). Coding of navigational distance in the visual scene-selective cortex. *Journal of Vision, 18*, 739. https://doi.org/10.1167/18.10.739

Park, S., Chun, M. M., & Johnson, M. K. (2010). Refreshing and integrating visual scenes in scene-selective cortex. *Journal of Cognitive Neuroscience, 22*(12), 2813–2822. https://doi.org/10.1162/jocn.2009.21406

Park, S., Intraub, H., Yi, D.-J., Widders, D., & Chun, M. M. (2007). Beyond the edges of a view: Boundary extension in human scene-selective visual cortex. *Neuron, 54*(2), 335–342. https://doi.org/10.1016/j.neuron.2007.04.006

Parker, R. (1978). Picture processing during recognition. *Journal of Experimental Psychology: Human Perception and Performance, 4*(2), 284–293.

Patihis, L., Frenda, S. J., & Loftus, E. F. (2018). False memory tasks do not reliably predict other false memories. *Psychology of Consciousness: Theory Research, and Practice, 5*(2), 140–160. https://doi.org/10.1037/cns0000147

Pennycook, G., & Rand, D. G. (2019). Lazy, not biased: Susceptibility to partisan fake news is better explained by lack of reasoning than by motivated reasoning. *Cognition, 188*, 39–50. https://doi.org/10.1016/j.cognition.2018.06.011

Pereira, E. J., & Castelhano, M. S. (2012). On-line contributions of peripheral information to visual search in scenes: Further explorations of object content and scene context. *Journal of Vision, 12*(9), 740. https://doi.org/10.1167/12.9.740

Pereira, E. J., & Castelhano, M. S. (2014). Peripheral guidance in scenes: The interaction of scene context and object content. *Journal of Experimental Psychology: Human Perception and Performance, 40*(5), 2056–2072. https://doi.org/10.1037/a0037524

Pereira, E. J., & Castelhano, M. S. (2019). Attentional capture is contingent on scene region: Using surface guidance framework to explore attentional mechanisms during search. *Psychonomic Bulletin & Review, 26*(4), 1273–1281. https://doi.org/10.3758/s13423-019-01610-z

Pieters, R., & Wedel, M. (2004). Attention capture and transfer in advertising: Brand, pictorial, and text-size effects. *Journal of Marketing, 68*(2), 36–50. https://doi.org/10.1509/jmkg.68.2.36.27794

Potter, M. C. (1976). Short-term conceptual memory for pictures. *Journal of Experimental Psychology: Human Learning and Memory, 2*(5), 509–522. https://doi.org/1003124

Potter, M. C., & Levy, E. I. (1969). Recognition memory for a rapid sequence of pictures. *Journal of Experimental Psychology, 81*(1), 10–15. https://doi.org/10.1037/h0027470

Powers, K. L., Brooks, P. J., Aldrich, N. J., Palladino, M. A., & Alfieri, L. (2013). Effects of video-game play on information processing: A meta-analytic investigation. *Psychonomic Bulletin & Review, 20*(6), 1055–1079. https://doi.org/10.3758/s13423-013-0418-z

Previc, F. H. (1998). The neuropsychology of 3-D space. *Psychological Bulletin, 124*(2), 123–164.

Price, C. J., & Humphreys, G. W. (1989). The effects of surface detail on object categorization and naming. *The Quarterly Journal of Experimental Psychology Section A, 41*(4), 797–828. https://doi.org/10.1080/14640748908402394

Radach, R., Lemmer, S., Vorstius, C., Heller, D., & Radach, K. (2003). Eye movements in the processing of print advertisements. In J. Hyönä, R. Radach, & H. Deubel (Eds.), *The mind's eye: Cognitive and applied aspects of eye movement research* (pp. 609–632). New York: Elsevier Inc. https://doi.org/10.1016/B978-044451020-4/50032-3

Rayner, K. (1975). The perceptual span and peripheral cues in reading. *Cognitive Psychology*, *7*(1), 65–81. https://doi.org/10.1016/0010-0285(75)90005-5

Rayner, K. (2009). Eye movements and attention in reading, scene perception, and visual search. *The Quarterly Journal of Experimental Psychology*, *62*(8), 1457–1506. https://doi.org/10.1080/17470210902816461

Rayner, K., & Castelhano, M. S. (2007a). Eye movements. *Scholarpedia*, *2*(10), 3649. https://doi.org/10.4249/scholarpedia.3649

Rayner, K., & Castelhano, M. S. (2007b). Eye movements during reading, scene perception, visual search, and while looking at print advertisements. *Visual Marketing from Attention to Action*, *2175*, 9–42. https://doi.org/10.4324/9780203809617

Rayner, K., & McConkie, G. W. (1976). What guides a reader's eye movements? *Vision Research*, *16*(8), 829–837. https://doi.org/10.1016/0042-6989(76)90143-7

Rayner, K., Castelhano, M. S., & Yang, J. (2009a). Eye movements and the perceptual span in older and younger readers. *Psychology and Aging*, *24*(3), 755–760. https://doi.org/10.1037/a0014300

Rayner, K., Castelhano, M. S., & Yang, J. (2009b). Eye movements when looking at unusual/weird scenes: Are there cultural differences? *Journal of Experimental Psychology: Learning, Memory, and Cognition*, *35*(1), 254–259. https://doi.org/10.1037/a0013508

Rayner, K., Castelhano, M. S., & Yang, J. (2010). Preview benefit during eye fixations in reading for older and younger readers. *Psychology and Aging*, *25*(3), 714–718. https://doi.org/10.1037/a0019199

Rayner, K., McConkie, G. W., & Ehrlich, S. (1978). Eye movements and integrating information across fixations. *Journal of Experimental Psychology: Human Perception and Performance*, *4*(4), 529–544. https://doi.org/10.1037/0096-1523.4.4.529

Rayner, K., Miller, B., & Rotello, C. M. (2008). Eye movements when looking at print advertisements: The goal of the viewer matters. *Wiley Online Library*, *22*(5), 697–707. https://doi.org/10.1002/acp.1389

Rayner, K., Li, X., Williams, C. C., Cave, K. R., & Well, A. D. (2007). Eye movements during information processing tasks: Individual differences and cultural effects. *Vision Research*, *47*(21), 2714–2726.

Rayner, K., Rotello, C. M., Stewart, A. J., Keir, J., & Duffy, S. A. (2001). Integrating text and pictorial information: Eye movements when looking at print advertisements. *Journal of Experimental Psychology: Applied, 7*(3), 219–226. https://doi.org/10.1037//1076-898x.7.3.219

Reed, W. M., Ryan, J. T., McEntee, M. F., Evanoff, M. G., & Brennan, P. C. (2011). The effect of abnormality-prevalence expectation on expert observer performance and visual search. *Radiology, 258*(3), 938–943. https://doi.org/10.1148/radiol.10101090

Reichle, E. D., Pollatsek, A., Fisher, D. L., & Rayner, K. (1998). Toward a model of eye movement control in reading. *Psychological Review, 105* (1), 125–157. https://doi.org/9450374

Reisz, K., & Millar, G. (1971). *The technique of film editing.* New York: Hastings House Publishers Inc.

Rensink, R. A. (2000). The dynamic representation of scenes. *Visual Cognition, 7*(1–3), 17–42.

Rensink, R. A., O'Regan, J. K., & Clark, J. J. (1997). To see or not to see: The need for attention to perceive changes in scenes. *Psychological Science, 8*(5), 368–373. https://doi.org/10.1111/j.1467-9280.1997.tb00427.x

Resnick, M., & Albert, W. (2014). The impact of advertising location and user task on the emergence of banner ad blindness: An eye-tracking study. *International Journal of Human-Computer Interaction, 30*(3), 206–219. https://doi.org/10.1080/10447318.2013.847762

Rizzolatti, G., Riggio, L., Dascola, I., & Umiltá, C. (1987). Reorienting attention across the horizontal and vertical meridians: Evidence in favor of a premotor theory of attention. *Neuropsychologia, 25*(1), 31–40. https://doi.org/10.1016/0028-3932(87)90041-8

Roediger, H. L. (1980). The effectiveness of four mnemonics in ordering recall. *Journal of Experimental Psychology: Human Learning & Memory, 6*(5), 558–567. https://doi.org/10.1037/0278-7393.6.5.558

Rogé, J., Pébayle, T., Lambilliotte, E., Spitzenstetter, F., Giselbrecht, D., & Muzet, A. (2004). Influence of age, speed and duration of monotonous driving task in traffic on the driver's useful visual field. *Vision Research, 44* (23), 2737–2744. https://doi.org/10.1016/j.visres.2004.05.026

Rolfs, M., Jonikaitis, D., Deubel, H., & Cavanagh, P. (2011). Predictive remapping of attention across eye movements. *Nature Neuroscience, 14*(2), 252–256. https://doi.org/10.1038/nn.2711

Roos, J. E., Paik, D., Olsen, D., Liu, E. G., Chow, L. C., Leung, A. N., Mindelzun, R., Choudhury, K. R., Naidich, D. P., Napel, S., & Rubin, G. D. (2010). Computer-aided detection (CAD) of lung nodules in CT scans: Radiologist performance and reading time with incremental CAD assistance. *European Radiology*, *20*(3), 549–557. https://doi.org/10.1007/s00330-009-1596-y

Rosenberg, R., & Klein, C. (2015). *The moving eye of the beholder: Eye tracking and the perception of paintings*. Oxford: Oxford University Press.

Rothkegel, L. O. M., Trukenbrod, H. A., Schütt, H. H., Wichmann, F. A., & Engbert, R. (2017). Temporal evolution of the central fixation bias in scene viewing. *Journal of Vision*, *17*(13), 3. https://doi.org/10.1167/17.13.3

Russell, B., Torralba, A., Murphy, K. P., & Freeman, W. T. (2008). LabelMe: A database and web-based tool for image annotation. *International Journal of Computer Vision*, *77*(1–3), 157–173.

Sanchez, C. A. (2012). Enhancing visuospatial performance through video game training to increase learning in visuospatial science domains. *Psychonomic Bulletin and Review*, *19*(1), 58–65. https://doi.org/10.3758/s13423-011-0177-7

Sanocki, T. (2003). Representation and perception of scenic layout. *Cognitive Psychology*, *47*(1), 43–86. https://doi.org/10.1016/S0010-0285(03)00002-1

Sanocki, T., & Epstein, W. (1997). Priming spatial layout of scenes. *Psychological Science*, *8*(5), 374–378. https://doi.org/10.1111/j.1467-9280.1997.tb00428.x

Schulman, A. I. (1973). Recognition memory and the recall of spatial location. *Memory & Cognition*, *1*(3), 256–260. https://doi.org/10.3758/BF03198106

Schyns, P. G., & Oliva, A. (1994). Evidence for time-and spatial-scale-dependent scene recognition. *Psychological Science*, *5*(4), 195–200.

Seltzer, S. E., Judy, P. F., Adams, D. F., Jacobson, F. L., Stark, P., Kikinis, R., Swensson, R. G., Hooton, S., Head, B., & Feldman, U. (1995). Spiral CT of the chest: Comparison of cine and film-based viewing. *Radiology*, *197*(1), 73–78. https://doi.org/10.1148/radiology.197.1.7568857

Serrano, A., Sitzmann, V., Ruiz-Borau, J., Wetzstein, G., Gutierrez, D., & Masia, B. (2017). Movie editing and cognitive event segmentation in virtual reality video. *ACM Transactions on Graphics*, *36*(4), 1–12. https://doi.org/10.1145/3072959.3073668

Shafer-Skelton, A., & Brady, T. F. (2019). Scene layout priming relies primarily on low-level features rather than scene layout. *Journal of Vision*, *19*(1), 14. https://doi.org/10.1167/19.1.14

Shepard, R. N. (1967). Recognition memory for words, sentences, and pictures. *Journal of Verbal Learning and Verbal Behavior*, *6*(1), 156–163. https://doi.org/10.1016/S0022-5371(67)80067-7

Simons, D., Chabris, C., Schnur, T., & Levin, D. (2002). Evidence for preserved representations in change blindness. *Consciousness and Cognition*, *11*(1), 78–97.

Smelter, T. J., & Calvillo, D. P. (2020). Pictures and repeated exposure increase perceived accuracy of news headlines. *Applied Cognitive Psychology, 34*, 1061–1071. https://doi.org/10.1002/acp.3684

Smith, T. J., & Martin-Portugues Santacreu, J. Y. (2017). Match-action: The role of motion and audio in creating global change blindness in film. *Media Psychology, 20*(2), 317–348. https://doi.org/10.1080/15213269 .2016.1160789

Smith, T. T. J., & Henderson, J. J. M. (2008). Edit blindness: The relationship between attention and global change blindness in dynamic scenes. *Journal of Eye Movement Research, 2*(2). https://doi.org/10.16910/jemr.2.2.6

Song, J., Bennett, P., Sekuler, A., & Sun, H.-J. (2017). Effect of apparent depth in peripheral target detection in driving under focused and divided attention. *Journal of Vision, 17*(10), 388. https://doi.org/10.1167/17.10.388

Spence, I., & Feng, J. (2010). Video games and spatial cognition. *Review of General Psychology, 14*(2), 92–104. https://doi.org/10.1037/a0019491

Spence, I., Wong, P., Rusan, M., & Rastegar, N. (2006). How color enhances visual memory for natural scenes. *Psychological Science, 17*(1), 1–6. https:// doi.org/10.1111/j.1467-9280.2005.01656.x

Spiers, H. J., & Maguire, E. A. (2007). A navigational guidance system in the human brain. *Hippocampus, 17*(8), 618–626. https://doi.org/10.1002/hipo.20298

Spinney, L. (2017). How Facebook, fake news and friends are warping your memory. *Nature, 543*(7644), 168–170. https://doi.org/10.1038/543168a

Spotorno, S., Malcolm, G. L., & Tatler, B. W. (2014). How context information and target information guide the eyes from the first epoch of search in real-world scenes. *Journal of Vision, 14*(2), 7. https://doi.org/10.1167/14.2.7

Spotorno, S., Tatler, B. W., & Faure, S. (2013). Semantic consistency versus perceptual salience in visual scenes: Findings from change detection. *Acta Psychologica, 142*(2), 168–176. https://doi.org/10.1016/J.ACTPSY.2012.12.009

Standing, L. (1973). Learning 10000 pictures. *Quarterly Journal of Experimental Psychology, 25*(2), 207–222. https://doi.org/10.1080 /14640747308400340

Standing, L., Conezio, J., & Haber, R. N. (1970). Perception and memory for pictures: Single-trial learning of 2500 visual stimuli. *Psychonomic Science, 19*(2), 73–74. https://doi.org/10.3758/BF03337426

Summerfield, J. J., Lepsien, J., Gitelman, D. R., Mesulam, M. M., & Nobre, A. C. (2006). Orienting attention based on long-term memory experience. *Neuron, 49*(6), 905–916. https://doi.org/10.1016/j.neuron.2006.01.021

Tanaka, J. W., & Presnell, L. M. (1999). Color diagnosticity in object recognition. *Perception and Psychophysics, 61*(6), 1140–1153. https://doi .org/10.3758/BF03207619

Tarr, M. J., & Pinker, S. (1989). Mental rotation and orientation-dependence in shape recognition. *Cognitive Psychology*, *21*(2), 233–282. https://doi.org/10.1016/0010-0285(89)90009-1

Tatler, B. W. (2007). The central fixation bias in scene viewing: Selecting an optimal viewing position independently of motor biases and image feature distributions. *Journal of Vision*, *7*(14), 4. https://doi.org/10.1167/7.14.4

Tatler, B. W., & Land, M. F. (2011). Vision and the representation of the surroundings in spatial memory. *Philosophical Transactions of the Royal Society B: Biological Sciences*, *366*(1564), 596–610. https://doi.org/10.1098/rstb.2010.0188

Tatler, B., Hayhoe, M., Land, M., & Ballard, D. (2011). Eye guidance in natural vision: Reinterpreting salience. *Journal of Vision*, *11*, 5.

Tatler, B. W., & Tatler, S. L. (2013). The influence of instructions on object memory in a real-world setting. *Journal of Vision*, *13*(2):5, 1–13.

Torralba, A., Oliva, A., Castelhano, M. S., & Henderson, J. M. (2006). Contextual guidance of eye movements and attention in real-world scenes: The role of global features in object search. *Psychological Review*, *113*(4), 766–786. https://doi.org/10.1037/0033-295X.113.4.766

Treisman, A., & Kahneman, D. (1984). Changing views of attention and automaticity. In R. Parasuraman & D. R. Davies (Eds.), *Varieties of attention* (pp. 29–61). New York: Academic Press.

Triesch, J., Ballard, D. H., Hayhoe, M. M., & Sullivan, B. T. (2003). What you see is what you need. *Journal of Vision*, *3*(1), 86–94. https://doi.org/10:1167/3.1.9

Tseng, P. H., Carmi, R., Cameron, I. G. M., Munoz, D. P., & Itti, L. (2009). Quantifying center bias of observers in free viewing of dynamic natural scenes. *Journal of Vision*, *9*(7), 4. https://doi.org/10.1167/9.7.4

Ullman, S. (1989). Aligning pictorial descriptions: An approach to object recognition. *Cognition*, *32*(3), 193–254. https://doi.org/10.1016/0010-0277(89)90036-X

Underwood, G., Humphreys, L., & Cross, E. (2007). Congruency, saliency and gist in the inspection of objects in natural scenes. *Eye Movements*, 563, 7. https://doi.org/10.1016/B978-008044980-7/50028-8

van der Lans, R., & Wedel, M. (2017). Eye movements during search and choice. *International Series in Operations Research and Management Science*, 254, 331–359. https://doi.org/10.1007/978-3-319-56941-3_11

Võ, Melissa L.-H., & Henderson, J. M. (2009). Does gravity matter? Effects of semantic and syntactic inconsistencies on the allocation of attention during scene perception. *Journal of Vision*, *9*(3), 24.1–15. https://doi.org/10.1167/9.3.24

Võ, Melissa L. -H., & Henderson, J. M. (2011). Object-scene inconsistencies do not capture gaze: Evidence from the flash-preview moving-window paradigm. *Attention, Perception & Psychophysics*, *73*(6), 1742–1753. https://doi.org/10.3758/s13414-011-0150-6

Võ, M. L. H., & Wolfe, J. M. (2013). Differential electrophysiological signatures of semantic and syntactic scene processing. *Psychological science*, 24(9), 1816–1823.

Võ, Melissa L.-H., Boettcher, S. E., & Draschkow, D. (2019). Reading scenes: How scene grammar guides attention and aids perception in real-world environments. *Current Opinion in Psychology*, *29*, 205–210. https://doi.org /10.1016/J.COPSYC.2019.03.009

Wade, K. A., Garry, M., Read, J. D., & Lindsay, D. S. (2002). A picture is worth a thousand lies: Using false photographs to create false childhood memories. *Psychonomic Bulletin and Review*, *9*(3), 597–603. https://doi.org/10.3758 /BF03196318

Waller, D., Friedman, A., Hodgson, E., & Greenauer, N. (2009). Learning scenes from multiple views: Novel views can be recognized more efficiently than learned views. *Memory & Cognition*, *37*(1), 90–99. https://doi.org/10 .3758/MC.37.1.90

Warren, W. H. (2012). Does this computational theory solve the right problem? Marr, Gibson, and the goal of vision. *Perception*, *41*(9), 1053–1060. https:// doi.org/10.1068/p7327

Wedel, M. (2017). Improving ad interfaces with eye tracking. In K. L. Norman and J. Kirakowski (Eds.), *The Wiley Handbook of Human Computer Interaction Set* (vol. 2, pp. 889–907). New York: Wiley. https://doi.org/10 .1002/9781118976005.ch41

Wedel, M., & Pieters, R. (2000). Eye fixations on advertisements and memory for brands: A model and findings. *Marketing Science*, *19*(4), 297–312. https://doi.org/10.1287/mksc.19.4.297.11794

Wichmann, F. A., Sharpe, L. T., & Gegenfurtner, K. R. (2002). The contributions of color to recognition memory for natural scenes. *Journal of Experimental Psychology: Learning Memory and Cognition*, *28*(3), 509–520. https://doi.org/10.1037/0278-7393.28.3.509

Williams, C. C. (2010). Incidental and intentional visual memory: What memories are and are not affected by encoding tasks? *Visual Cognition*, *18*(9), 1348–1367. https://doi.org/10.1080/13506285.2010.486280

Williams, C. C. (2020). Looking for your keys: The interaction of attention, memory, and eye movements in visual search. In K. Federmeier & E. R. Schotter (Eds.), *Gazing toward the future: Advances in eye movement theory and applications* (p. 195). New York: Academic Press.

Williams, C. C., & Castelhano, M. S. (2019). The changing landscape: High-level influences on eye movement guidance in scenes. *Vision*, *3*(3), 33. https://doi.org/10.3390/vision3030033

Williams, C. C., Zacks, R. T., & Henderson, J. M. (2009). Age differences in what is viewed and remembered in complex conjunction search. *Quarterly Journal of Experimental Psychology*, *62*(5), 946–966. https://doi.org/10.1080/17470210802321976

Williams, L. H., & Drew, T. (2019). What do we know about volumetric medical image interpretation? A review of the basic science and medical image perception literatures. *Cognitive Research: Principles and Implications*, *4*(1), 1–24. https://doi.org/10.1186/s41235-019-0171-6

Wirth, S., Baraduc, P., Planté, A., Pinède, S., & Duhamel, J. R. (2017). Gaze-informed, task-situated representation of space in primate hippocampus during virtual navigation. *PLoS Biology*, *15*(2), e2001045. https://doi.org/10.1371/journal.pbio.2001045

Wolfe, J. M. (2007). Guided search 4.0. In Wayne D. Gray (Ed.), *Integrated models of cognitive systems* (pp. 99–119). Oxford: Oxford University Press.

Wolfe, J. M., Alaoui Soce, A., & Schill, H. M. (2017). How did I miss that? Developing mixed hybrid visual search as a "model system" for incidental finding errors in radiology. *Cognitive Research: Principles and Implications*, *2*(1), 1–10. https://doi.org/10.1186/s41235-017-0072-5

Wolfe, J. M., Horowitz, T. S., & Kenner, N. M. (2005). Rare items often missed in visual searches. *Nature*, *435*(7041), 439–440. https://doi.org/10.1038/435439a

Wolfe, J. M., Evans, K. K., Drew, T., Aizenman, A., & Josephs, E. (2016). How do radiologists use the human search engine? *Radiation Protection Dosimetry*, *169*(1), 24–31. https://doi.org/10.1093/rpd/ncv501

Wolfe, J. M., Horowitz, T. S., Van Wert, M. J., Kenner, N. M., Place, S. S., & Kibbi, N. (2007). Low target prevalence is a stubborn source of errors in visual search tasks. *Journal of Experimental Psychology: General*, *136*(4), 623–638. https://doi.org/10.1037/0096-3445.136.4.623

Wu, S., Cheng, C. K., Feng, J., D'Angelo, L., Alain, C., & Spence, I. (2012). Playing a first-person shooter video game induces neuroplastic change. *Journal of Cognitive Neuroscience*, *24*(6), 1–8. https://doi.org/10.1162/jocn_a_00192

Yao, A. Y. J., & Einhauser, W. (2008). Color aids late but not early stages of rapid natural scene recognition. *Journal of Vision*, *8*(16), 12–12. https://doi.org/10.1167/8.16.12

Yarbus, A. L. (1967). *Eye movements and vision*. New York: Springer. https://doi.org/10.1007/978-1-4899-5379-7

Zelinsky, G. J. (2008). A theory of eye movements during target acquisition. *Psychological Review*, *115*(4), 787–835. https://doi.org/2008-14936-011

Zelinsky, G. J., & Loschky, L. C. (2005). Eye movements serialize memory for objects in scenes. *Perception & Psychophysics*, *67*(4), 676–690. https://doi.org/10.3758/bf03193524

Zelinsky, G. J., Chen, Y., Ahn, S., & Adeli, H. (2020). Changing perspectives on goal-directed attention control: The past, present, and future of modeling fixations during visual search. In K. D. Federmeier & E. R. Schotter (Eds.), *Gazing toward the future: Advances in eye movement theory and applications* (pp. 231–286). New York: Academic Press. https://doi.org/10.1016/bs.plm.2020.08.001

Zelinsky, G. J., Rao, R. P. N., Hayhoe, M. M., & Ballard, D. H. (1997). Eye movements reveal the spatiotemporal dynamics of visual search. *Psychological Science*, *8*(6), 448–453. https://doi.org/10.1111/j.1467-9280.1997.tb00459.x

Zhao, M., Gersch, T. M., Schnitzer, B. S., Dosher, B. A., & Kowler, E. (2012). Eye movements and attention: The role of pre-saccadic shifts of attention in perception, memory and the control of saccades. *Vision Research*, *74*, 40–60. https://doi.org/10.1016/J.VISRES.2012.06.017

Cambridge Elements ☰

Perception

James T. Enns
The University of British Columbia

Editor James T. Enns is Professor at the University of British Columbia, where he researches the interaction of perception, attention, emotion, and social factors. He has previously been Editor of the *Journal of Experimental Psychology: Human Perception and Performance* and an Associate Editor at *Psychological Science, Consciousness and Cognition, Attention Perception & Psychophysics,* and *Visual Cognition.*

Editorial Board

About the Series
The modern study of human perception includes event perception, bidirectional influences between perception and action, music, language, the integration of the senses, human action observation, and the important roles of emotion, motivation, and social factors. Each Element in the series combines authoritative literature reviews of foundational topics with forward-looking presentations of the recent developments on a given topic.

Cambridge Elements ⹀

Perception

Elements in the Series

A full series listing is available at: www.cambridge.org/EPER

Printed in the United States
by Baker & Taylor Publisher Services